PENGUIN

Shoe Money

Maggie Alderson was born in London, brought up in Staffordshire and educated at the University of St Andrews. She has worked on nine magazines and two newspapers and was editor of *ELLE* in London and *Mode* in Sydney. She is now a senior writer with *The Sydney Morning Herald* and her weekly column 'Style Notes' appears in the *Good Weekend*. She had over seventy pairs of shoes at last count.

Shoe money

with illustrations by the author

Maggie Alderson

PENGUIN BOOKS

Penguin Books Australia Ltd
487 Maroondah Highway, PO Box 257
Ringwood, Victoria 3134, Australia
Penguin Books Ltd
Harmondsworth, Middlesex, England
Penguin Putnam Inc.
375 Hudson Street, New York, New York 10014, USA
Penguin Books Canada Limited
10 Alcorn Avenue, Toronto, Ontario, Canada M4V 3B2
Penguin Books (NZ) Ltd
Cnr Rosedale and Airborne Roads, Albany, Auckland, New Zealand
Penguin Books (South Africa) (Pty) Ltd
4 Pallinghurst Road, Parktown 2193, South Africa

First published by Penguin Books Australia Ltd 1998

5 7 9 10 6 4

Cover photo: shoe by Manolo Blahnik, courtesy of Evelyn Miles
Design by Debra Billson, Penguin Design Studio
Typeset in 12.5/16pt Perpetua by Post Pre-press Group, Brisbane
Printed in Australia by Australian Print Group, Maryborough, Victoria

National Library of Australia
Cataloguing-in-Publication data:

Alderson, Maggie.
Shoe money.

ISBN 0 14 027967 9.

1. Fashion – Australia – Humor. 2. Life style – Australia – Humor.
3. Australian wit and humor.
I. Title.

391.00207

This book is dedicated to my grandmother,
Peg Mackay, and my mother, Peggy Alderson.
Two very stylish girls.

CONTENTS

Shoe me the money

Isn't it funny how some dollars are worth more than others? It works like dog years. Dollars spent on shoes are worth about twenty cents, whereas in household-appliance money, $1 is equal to $50. We'll call it Shoe Money.

This is why I think nothing of spitting out $150 for a pair of sandals, but resent every cent of the $40 a new toaster is going to cost me. I'll shop around for weeks, consulting consumer guides and making toast over a candle, before I shell out for a toaster, but I'll buy those sandals entirely by accident when I really went out for some asparagus.

This is because, when you do your conversions, the sandals cost only $30 in Shoe Money, whereas that silly old toaster – which I can't even wear – is going to cost $2000 in real terms.

No matter that I will use the toaster every day of my life for the next twenty years and will wear the sandals twice, getting hideous blisters and shin splints on both occasions.

Toasters are boring. They should be free.

Unless you have one of those very pretentious chrome American diner things, your toaster isn't going to impress anyone, and those things cost the equivalent of about two pairs of stilettos. And that's without putting it into Shoe Money.

Mind you, not all household items are boring. Saucepans are clothes — saucepans are fashion. If you buy well, they're shiny and have status value. Cheap aluminium pans say as much about a person's self-esteem as cheap shoes. Low. And cheap shoes don't even give you Alzheimer's. For all these reasons, I was happy to divert quite a few shoe dollars towards a beautiful trio of stainless-steel pans. I was also able to justify it to myself using the argument that I would Always Have Them, so they were Worth It.

You can use a similar argument for spending half the national debt on one jacket. It's called the Cost Per Wear system. By this logic (dreamed up, no doubt, by a collective of international designers), a $1200 jacket that you wear 1200 times really costs you $1, whereas a $200 jacket worn twice costs $100. See? Armani is cheap. You're dumb if you don't buy it. Buy two, save more.

Then there is the Appropriate Attire System. Working to this philosophy, you are quite entitled to buy new clothes for any upcoming event because you don't have anything suitable to wear. It doesn't matter that it could be fifteen years before you next go to a point-to-point in Scotland, you were correctly dressed that one time and it would have been rude not to be. It also doesn't matter how much the outfit costs, because you had to be suitably dressed and they just don't happen to sell Barbour jackets at Dotti. In other words, it wasn't your fault – the dress code made you do it.

All evening wear works according to this principle, and it really is the biggest rip-off of all time. I suggest you team and tone some simple black separates and dress them up with that chrome toaster you were foolish enough to buy.

Then you can spend what you save on shoes.

Saucepans are clothes - saucepans are fashion

Tantric shampooing

Next time you are having your hair washed at the salon and a teenage boy is confusing your head with a football as he administers the 'relaxing' head massage, take your mind off the pain by considering this true story.

At a hairdresser's I used to go to in London there was an eighteen-year-old apprentice called Agidio. Aaaaaaaah, Agidio. Just the sound of his name brings back the sensation of bands of fairies having group sex on my scalp.

I don't know what it was about Agidio. With your eyes open he was rather a skinny specimen, but close them and he was the Casanova of conditioner. Ah ah ah Agidio . . . This was tantric shampooing.

The lightest touch of his fingers had the hairdresser's normally poised Knightsbridge clientele quivering and moaning as he lathered them up at the backwash. According to salon legend, one woman actually had a fully fledged headgasm right there in the middle of the wash 'n' blow-dry area.

Certainly I have it on good authority that I came round from my first Agidio shampoo scarlet to the ear tips. After having the same experience the week before, my best friend was so astonished she came in specially to watch me — she wanted to make sure it wasn't just her.

She needn't have worried. It quickly became apparent that the shampoo Svengali of SW1 worked the same magic on everyone. We became a kind of unspoken sisterhood, and total strangers would nudge each other and wink as another unknowing initiate was led to Agidio's basin.

I could never decide whether this callow youth actually knew the effect he was having on us all, but I suspect he did. Surely no-one could do this by accident. For when Agidio touched your head, choirs of seraphim sang the *Hallelujah* chorus and golden lambs gambolled through your follicles. For an all-too-brief interlude, his fingers and your scalp felt like one. He was Keith Richards, you were the guitar string. He was Miles Davis, you were the trumpet. He was Neil Perry, you were the onion.

He must have been doing it on purpose. But after the conditioner was washed out it was hard to look him in the eye. You knew you were just another notch on his nozzle.

He was Italian, after all.

Word about Agidio quickly got round the thrill-hungry career-shopping set, and women of all ages used to request him particularly when they rang up to book their hairdos. (I'm sure I wasn't the only one.) You could see the

5

receptionist stifling her giggles when yet another client called up, saying, 'I don't care who cuts it, sweetie, but I'd like that nice Italian boy to wash it, please.' By the end of each day his jeans were bulging with tips. And quite a few phone numbers.

But, sadly, it was our bankable gratitude which spelled the end of bubbly bliss in Beauchamp Place. One summer Agidio spent the loot on a plane ticket to the Amalfi coast and never came back.

Rumour has it there is a wealthy Italian widow living somewhere near Positano with a big smile on her face and very clean hair.

The clothes I love
so much I can't
wear them

You should see my new coat. It's a beauty. Wool and cashmere, camel-coloured, just to the knee and tailored like something Prince Charles wore when he was four, but without the velvet collar.

Well, it's not that new any more actually. I've had it six months, but it's still new to me because I haven't exactly worn it yet. Well, not out of the house anyway.

Every time I put my new coat on I feel like an heiress. I feel like a princess. I feel like Carolyn Bessette Kennedy. I feel like that for a bit and then I take it straight off and put it back in the cupboard on my best padded hanger. It's too nice to *wear*. If I wore it, it would get spoiled. Then I wouldn't have my Beautiful New

7

Coat any more. It would just be another coat.

The problem is that you can't wear your beautiful new clothes and have them.

I was going to wear BNC the other day; I had the whole outfit worked out, with my delicious blue suede knee-boots (which I've never worn outside either) and some nifty scarf action. I felt pretty special. But when I got outside it looked like rain, and I was only going to work, so I went back home and put on my old raincoat and some nasty old shoes. I couldn't waste camel coat's maiden voyage on such a banal occasion.

Of course, I can remember when old raincoat was beautiful new raincoat, with its luxuriant fake-fur collar and thrilling swing cut. Now it's just That Old Thing. And you know how that happened. I wore it.

Sometimes I wear Supercoat around the house, just so I can swish past a few mirrors and accidentally notice myself. What a beautiful coat you're wearing. Why, thank you. It's French. I bought it in London. How marvellous. You must be so proud. Yes, we're very happy.

I was going to wear it one night when I was going out for dinner with some very chic people, but I realised at my front door that the restaurant wouldn't have a padded hanger to put it on. The thought of BNC being dangled from a distorting peg, or thrown over a chair with other coats that it hadn't been introduced to, was too awful. So I wore a slightly sad leather jacket instead, which has never been the same since it got caught in a rainstorm at the zoo.

Of course, some things get better with wear. Fortunes have been made making new clothes look like a teenage boy took them camping and then Grandma washed them on the whites cycle.

And no English aristocrat would set brogue on the grouse moors in tweeds that hadn't been in the family for several generations. I went to university in Scotland with boys called Hamish and Angus who swaggered around in their great-grandfathers' kilts. Nobody ever laughed at them, but oh how we snickered at American exchange students attempting the reel of the Fifty-first Division in recently minted plaid.

Which is all very well, but the hard bit is getting your gear from gorgeous new to dear old friend. There is a ghastly stage in the middle, rather like adolescence, where the clothes don't look new, or delightfully weathered. They just look sullen and spotty.

But not my camel coat. BNC is staying safely at home until we can guarantee an occasion where it will be fully appreciated and can be worn for several hours in a standing position.

Probably some time next June.

Hats off to hats

Hats are great. They hide your hair on the days it goes on strike. They keep the cruel fingernails of UV off your forehead. They make short people taller. They add character to the plainest attire. They break the ice at parties.

It's just a shame you feel such a git wearing one.

I've got acres of hats. I've got so many I use a pile of hat-boxes as a bedside table. I've had impromptu hat parties for thirty people without having to phone out for supplies.

My hall coat stand is covered with hats. Covered with hats covered with dust. I mean to wear them, I really do, but every time I put one on and go to walk out the door I feel overcome by shame.

It's like parading around with a banner saying, 'Hey, I'm kooky and fun to be with!' and, 'You don't have to be boring to wear this hat, but it helps!'

Hats are like bow ties, only bigger.

It's not just that I would like to see some return on the

hundreds of dollars, drachmas, bahts, francs and punts I've spent on the stupid, goofy things. In this climate we really need hats.

But while most of us happily slip and slop, we just can't seem to get into the slap. It's damned foolish, because hats are the nearest thing we have to an ozone layer in this country. But check out a city street on a sunny day and you'll find it largely a hat-free zone. The only place you'll see large gatherings of headgear here is at the Melbourne Cup or a dermatologists' convention.

Of course, it's different out in the bush. Everybody wears hats out there. Even people from Sydney. I felt quite normal strutting around Darwin and Katherine and Byron Bay in my straw stetson, and I've worn a hat in Noosa and on Bondi Beach without blushing, but there's still something impossibly cringey about wearing one in the CBD.

And by the way, baseball caps aren't hats. They're clothes; they're head T-shirts; they're just stuff. They're so ubiquitous we don't see them any more. That's the stage we need to reach with proper hats. Things with crowns and wide brims need to look as normal as a polyester suit in Pitt Street mall.

The only way this is going to happen is if we all start wearing the things. Every day and everywhere. All of us. But until you all join in, I guess I'll carry on walking around holding a newspaper to my forehead.

Now that looks daft.

In the name of Rose

This is the story of a silk stocking. Once upon a time there was a young journalist who lived in a rent-controlled flat in the London neighbourhood of Covent Garden. (All right, it was me, I'm just trying to get you in the mood.)

The flat was in a Queen Anne revival building in a paved courtyard lined with trees, right opposite the Royal Opera House. The old Bow Street police station was on the corner and Eliza Doolittle's market buildings were just down the road. It was a very special place, but the best part about it was my next-door neighbour.

Rose was eighty-one years old and she had lived in that apartment since she was one. Before that, she lived in a flat on the ground floor of the building, which was built just before she was born. She was a Covent Garden gal and she found the sudden changes to the area bewildering.

She couldn't understand why, in 1986, it was so hard to

find a packet of caustic soda nearby. Why weren't there any grocers any more?

A tiny slip of a person, Rose was very pretty. She wore her hair in a flapper bob and she never went out without a hat, a coat, gloves and lipstick, her handbag over her arm. She had cornflower-blue eyes. And whenever I introduced her to friends of the young, handsome male variety, she would noticeably twinkle. They all fell immediately in love.

Rose had lived alone since her sister died and I would go and watch *Dynasty* with her to give her a bit of company. It was her favourite programme because of 'the gowns'. Rose knew about quality. She had been a manicurist in the grand hotels of London from the 1920s onwards and she would tell me about all the fine ladies who came to her. Film stars and everything.

Of course, you didn't speak to your betters in those days, Rose explained. But they used to speak to her. Oh, the things they told her!

Occasionally, an elegantly dressed older gentleman would come to the flat for a manicure. I think he really came because he liked seeing Rose, but she still enjoyed getting her orange stick out. She had beautiful nails herself and she told me that the secret was to rub a little bit of grease into your cuticles every night. That was all you had to do. I still do it.

One evening I went to pay Rose a visit and nodded off in front of her gas fire and Krystle Carrington. The reason I was so tired, I explained, was because I had been out dancing the night before.

Where did you go? asked Rose.

The Café de Paris.

I used to go there, she said. In fact, I danced with the Prince of Wales at the Café de Paris. Not this one. The one before him.

Did you really? How wonderful.

Oh, no, it wasn't. He was a horrible man. He was drunk. He laddered my stocking. Would you like to see it?

Rose disappeared off to her bedroom and came back with a fine, flesh-coloured silk stocking, carefully folded in a linen envelope. She took it out and showed me. There was a big ladder right where your shin would be.

One morning I knocked on Rose's door and there was no reply. I ran to Bow Street police station and a bobby came and broke the lock. Rose had died in the night. And a little piece of London died with her.

Straight after her funeral, property developers stripped her apartment and tricked it up like a whore's boudoir (shortly before they managed to get me and all the other tenants out of the building).

I always wonder what happened to that stocking.

The great fashion myths

Fashion myth: Vertical stripes are flattering.

Vertical stripes are not flattering. As any deckchair will tell you. Yes, they do initially make the eye move up and down the body, but then they make it move backwards and forwards across it, counting exactly how many stripes it takes to cover your form.

Then the eye registers that it takes a heck of a lot more stripes to cover your torso than it does to cover Gwyneth Paltrow's.

Vertical stripes also have a charming way of drawing attention to gaping buttons and all the places where the fabric is pulled out of shape by your voluptuous curves.

And they announce loudly to passers-by, 'I am wearing vertical stripes to make myself look thinner.'

Fashion fact: Black is flattering and does not show where your body is testing the tensile strength of a fabric.

Fashion myth: You should accentuate your good points with light colours.

This reasoning leads directly to that old-favourite tip that pear-shaped women should attract attention to their teeny-tiny upper bodies by wearing pale colours on top and darker colours on their big fat bottoms, so that no-one will notice them.

In fact, this has the effect of making the slender area look bigger, so that the good point becomes a not-so-good point and they just look like soncy lassies from head to toe.

Fashion fact: Black clothes make all parts of the body look slimmer.

Fashion myth: The white shirt is a wardrobe essential.

Well, first there is the laundering, and even when you have washed, starched and ironed the stupid thing, the bus ride to work will turn what was supposed to 'add crispness and lighten your face' into an old tea towel with grey cuffs.

I once worked with a woman who would re-iron her white shirt each lunchtime at the gym, to hold on to that crispy feeling. That's twice a day. Is that really what you want to spend your time doing?

Then there is the way you spend all day tucking it back into your trousers, or else look like an Austrian blind with legs. Something about the shape of men's bodies seems to keep their shirts tucked in, while women's ruck up and go nasty.

Not to mention the unsightly bulges caused by the excess fabric that you have to stash away among your own unsightly bulges. Of course, Donna Karan invented the 'body' shirt, with joined-on panties, to combat exactly these problems. Which is a great idea if you are nostalgic for the feeling of full nappies.

Fashion fact: Donna Karan also does a great line in black jersey shirts which don't need ironing, don't show dirt and don't need tucking in.

Fashion myth: Jeans are comfortable and great for travel.

There is such a thing as comfortable jeans. But to be comfortable, they must also be slightly too big – perfect if you want to give the impression you have parked your Harley just around the corner while you pop out for another quick piercing.

Flattering jeans are too small and not recommended for those prone to crotch claustrophobia. People who wear jeans on long-haul flights should be given some kind of endurance medal. Denim also weighs more than lead and smells hamsterish after one wearing. Leave them at home.

Fashion fact: Black pants made from cotton with Lycra are flattering and comfortable, weigh next to nothing and keep their shape from Sydney to Rome. And still fit on the way home.

Blonde faith

Blondes have less fun.

Of course, it depends on your definition of fun. If you love nothing better than a wet T-shirt competition, pole dancing and having 'Hey Big Tits!' shouted at you in the street, you will definitely have more opportunities as a blonde.

But if your idea of a good time is a four-hour foreign-language movie followed by dinner at an interesting new Korean restaurant, you're going to be spending a lot of nights in, Pamela.

Teenage boys and yobbos love blondes. Gentlemen prefer brunettes. I can't say I blame them. I used to think Roger Daltrey was the most gorgeous man on earth (it was the 1970s) until I saw *The Godfather* and blond men ceased to exist. Al Pacino's glossy black hair changed the shape of the world for me.

It's the same for intelligent men. They were mad about

Debbie Harry until they saw Anouk Aimee in *A Man and a Woman* and it was all over red rover for us blondies.

There is no doubt dark is the more sophisticated choice. Blondes are Babycham, brunettes are brandy. Blondes are Tip Top, brunettes are sourdough. Right now, I bet Prince William has Pamela Anderson and Claudia Schiffer all over his Eton study walls. But he'll grow out of it. He'll see *Breakfast at Tiffany's* and never look at another blonde again.

Well, he will look at them. We stand out more. He'll look at them, he may well shout 'Show us your growler!' at a few, and, considering how devastatingly handsome he is (even for a blond), he'll probably bed several thousand of them.

But he won't fall in love with one.

Men feel romantic only about brunettes. They feel horny about blondes but they don't write us poetry – they don't think we're intelligent enough to understand it.

When I was at university, I dyed my hair from Diana Dors bottle-blonde to Siouxsie Sioux coal-black one evening (anything rather than work on my essay). Overnight, my marks went up. One art history tutor who used to look through me in tutorials suddenly treated all my contributions with the utmost respect. Even the ones about how Bellini's Christs were more attractive than Giotto's.

After a few months, I tired of looking like an extra from *Night of the Zombie Flesh Eaters* and cut it all off, to grow back natural. With every additional centimetre of fair to middling hair, people's expectations of my IQ retreated.

Fifteen years later, I still cop 'dumb blonde' prejudice. Occasionally, intelligent, interesting men who meet me in the dark when I'm wearing a hat accidentally ask me out. Sooner or later they always tell me, 'You're the first blonde I've ever been out with . . .' (To which one added, winningly, 'But you've got a brunette brain.')

No doubt they were concerned I might think they were the kind of guys who liked blondes, and think less of them.

They'd be right.

Shopping with Kate Moss

I once went shopping with Kate Moss. And we're not talking just looking, thank you. I tried things on next to her — in a communal changing room.

So there we were trying things on and she was looking at how she looked in them and I was looking at how I looked in them and I suddenly felt rather thoughtful and deeply regretted that I didn't have my degree certificate with me to show her.

'You look great in that size-six sausage skin, Kate,' I might have said. 'I've got an M.A., you know. What is the capital of Peru?'

But the spooky thing was that, after trying on just about everything agnès b. had to offer (we were in Paris, I was following her around during the couture shows, somebody had to), and after much consideration, we both bought a pair of trousers. The same pair of trousers. Well, there were two pairs, actually, but we both bought the same style.

Now, I am 152.5 cm tall and definitely not a super-model, but those trousers made me feel chic, *soignée* and generally super. And they looked pretty good on her too. True, I had to have about six inches cut off the legs of mine and they weren't quite exactly the same size as hers to begin with (Kate's were very slightly smaller), but still they were exactly the same cut of trouser.

It wasn't a freak event, either. Another time I went to the Joseph sale in London with a 19-year-old junior fashion editor who strongly resembled a walking French bean. I was a 26-year-old features editor who strongly resembled a piano stool. We bought the same Azzedine Alaïa dress.

Nothing more complicated than a little slip of black Lycra, it pulled her waist in, pushed her mozzie-bite boo-bies out and curved her formica-flat behind into something more akin to Jessica Rabbit than her usual skinned rabbit. The same dress pulled my waist in, flattened my tummy and offered my bottie and bosom up like food for the gods. Or whoever else happened to be around.

We looked at each other in amazement and rushed for the cash desk. From then on we referred to them as The Magic Dresses. How I wish I had bought two and laid one down to mature. Because after years in action as the ulti-mate party frock – dress it up, dress it down, take it off – the Lycra began to sag, the black faded to charcoal and The

Magic Dress begged to be retired. It couldn't bear to dance on one more table. I consigned it to a clothing bin with tears in my eyes.

Since that day I must have tried on 150 little black Lycra dresses in an effort to replace it. No dice. They have variously pushed my stomach out, flattened my chest, squidged my bottom and made me feel about as attractive as a McDonald's uniform.

There are several morals to this tale:

1. If an item of clothing makes you look hideous and misshapen, it's not your fault. It's the designer's fault. A really good cut suits everybody. Quasimodo would have felt quite differently about himself in an Alaïa dress.

2. Jackie Onassis was right. If a garment makes you instantly feel like a sexy Parisienne swinging down the avenue, buy two and save one for later.

3. Shop in Paris.

Boys of summer

This one is for the boys. There is something we have to tell you. We hate your short-sleeved shirts. They may very well be practical under a suit for hot summer days, but they make your arms look stringy and weird and we want your arms to look knotty and strong.

We particularly hate them with ties, because you remind us of maths teachers who made us do long division on the blackboard in front of the whole class ('Carry three, okay. Er . . . where?'). And they make you look like Mormons, which might be fine if we were still hung up on little Donny Osmond, but actually we preferred David Cassidy, because he rolled his sleeves up.

Rolled-up sleeves are dreamy. Just above the wrist they are the Flying Doctor about to do an emergency tonsillectomy in the bush. Cranked up to the bicep they are a smouldering mechanic about to do an emergency knickerectomy in a panel van. So don't get the shears to them boys – roll 'em, roll 'em, roll 'em.

But even more than those awful amputated business shirts, the menswear summer staple we completely and utterly loathe are those printed viscose fun shirts you wear at the weekend. They are so scruffy and unconvincing and something about those horrid muddy patterns makes the hair on your arms look dirty. We hate the sprouty open necks and the way the sleeves stick out and look dorky. One wash and they are a dishcloth. No amount of pressing can put life back into those rags. Bin them. Please. Stamp on them, call them names, set fire to them and then bin them.

There is, however, one kind of short sleeve which we find acceptable in gentlemen's warm-weather attire. That is the ribbing-edged short sleeve of the polo shirt. It's all to do with physics. The slight puffing effect caused by the narrow band of ribbing on the cotton pique jersey makes even the scrawniest shoulder look plump and luscious.

And on a man with a fine physique, like – oh I don't know, a bronzed, sweating Argentinian polo player with his Moon in Aries and little gold flecks in his green eyes and shiny boots and a Breitling watch and a tattoo of a tiger on his . . . anyway, the effect is extremely erogenous. Even Prince Charles looks sexy in a polo shirt (as long as you put a bag over his head).

But beware – those pretend polo shirts in smooth jersey with sticky-out nerd sleeves which people wear to play golf do not count, and should be banned by an act of parliament. Although, bizarrely, a very toffy Sydney golf club actually stipulates in its rule book that only flappy short sleeves can be worn on their greens.

The section starts something like, 'No sexually attractive clothing to be worn on Club premises. Members must look repulsive at all times. Nasty short-sleeved shirts, emerald-green plaid trousers and two-tone shoes preferred for tournaments.' Well, that's one club I'm very glad doesn't want me as a member.

rolled-up
sleeves are
dreamy

So that's the scoop, fellas. If you want to impress the chicks this summer, throw out the viscose and make Ralph Lauren a bit richer. And if you stick to your side of the bargain, we promise we'll stop wearing leggings and big T-shirts. Deal?

Emotional baggage

Packing has a lot in common with method acting. Both require the mental exertion of re-experiencing powerful sense memories. And you'll look like a total twit if you get either of them wrong.

Assembling my neat capsule wardrobe for a forthcoming trip to Greece, I stand in my bedroom wearing a sundress and woolly socks, trying to remember what it feels like to trudge around piles of rubble in oxyacetylene sunshine.

The sundress stays, and a light shirt, a water bottle and a fold-up hat get added to the growing pyramid of essential items. Lee Strasberg would be proud of me as I move on to the next exercise – summoning up the sensations of sitting outside a taverna with a brisk breeze blowing off the Aegean, wishing I'd packed a cardigan. On to the pile it goes. And more socks.

It's not a bad system for packing – better than those hilarious American catalogues which offer uncrushable blazers that fold down to the size of a pack of cards and uncrushable trousers which unzip into uncrushable shorts, with special clips from which to hang the unwanted lower legs. Hi! My name's Marvin! I'm from Baltimore. Hot enough for ya?

The only problem with method packing is that if you pursue it with vigour you actually start believing you're someone else. As Marlon Brando would tell you.

Moving through my holiday scenarios, I can feel the soft caress of my skimpy summer dress as I breeze along a dusty Greek lane, my taut, brown arms swinging a brightly coloured raffia bag. The bag will love the outing; it was bought in a moment of premenstrual madness and hasn't been out since, because I feel like a pretentious prat holding it.

But the Holiday Me loves that krazee bag. She also cunningly uses a tangle of brightly coloured scarves to dress up her simple co-ordinating outfits and feels confident going out in public with bare arms. Holiday Me pushes back her cuticles (well, there must be a reason there's always an orange stick in my toilet bag when I get there) and enjoys Booker Prize-nominated novels. Which is why she always packs three of them and then Real Me has to shell out the equivalent of $30 for a Jilly Cooper paperback on day two.

Holiday Me rinses out her undies each night (why waste space taking more than one pair? she asks briskly) and hangs them to dry on her travel clothes line, rather than wearing the same ones for three days before abandoning them altogether.

And Holiday Me seems to spend a great deal of her time lingering languorously around in long slip dresses, watching the sun sink into the ocean on perfect balmy evenings.

Her arms never get bitten by sandflies while she is doing it, so she never thinks to throw in the calamine lotion.

One drawback is that Holiday Margaret tends to have quite a bit of luggage because she wears several different outfits every day (probably to get into character), whereas the Real Margaret soon discovers that, away from peer pressure, she is quite happy to wear the same clothes for a week, just adding layers like sedimentary rock.

So you'll never see me waltzing past the baggage carousel with my neat carry-on bag. I'll be the one shouldering a vast kitbag of assumed identities. Maybe one day I'll get an Oscar for Best Supporting Wardrobe.

Carry on packing

Well, I'm back from Greece now. In the end I didn't take it all with me, because a chance remark by a friend shamed me into travelling the carry-on way. 'You're just bringing a little in-flight bag, of course,' she said. 'We don't want to be hanging around the airport waiting for you. We never check our luggage.' So, to avoid total humiliation, I thought I'd better give it a go.

What this carry-on malarkey actually means is cramming your possessions into one small but incredibly heavy squashy bag which you then have to lug around the airport like Sherpa Tenzing (or Sherpa Clarins, as my friend Sebastian calls himself on holiday).

It might feel really super at the other end as you sweep straight from the plane and snare the only taxi on the rank, while everyone else waits for the baggage handlers to finish their afternoon siesta, but it really gets in the way of those pre-flight airport pleasures, let me tell you.

Airport shopping is often the best part of a holiday as far as I am concerned. Being in transit seems to bring out some kind of latent insecurity which makes me want to buy everything in sight. Obviously I am not the only one with this affliction. Some of the best shopping in Sydney is at the International Terminal, and London's Gatwick Airport is a huge shopping mall with runways attached. You can buy things like lawn-mowers there.

Cruising novelty chocolate shops, buying a second Walkman because it seems rude not to, stocking up on a bit more duty-free Clarins, fourteen fashion magazines and three more Booker-nominated doorstops, just in case you tear through the others in the first week, is all part of the process.

If you're doing the carry-on thing, you then add all these new possessions to your already considerable burden so that you approach the departure gate resembling a biblical donkey. Then you have to cram it all under the seat in front of you, because someone else has already filled the over-head storage space with their in-flight baggage, while you were still looking feverishly at the chocolate macadamia nut koalas.

On domestic flights in America, where they are much more lenient about the size of bags and how many you can take into the cabin, everyone uses those trolley cases and carry-on suitpacks. Nobody checks their luggage. It can be quite hard getting to your seat climbing over all the

Christmas trees, Thanksgiving turkeys, shoe trunks and lawn-mowers. The holds on those planes must be completely empty. It's a miracle they don't fly upside down.

It doesn't get better. Once you reach the other end and have unbuckled your lower limbs, you then have to lug your friend the carry-on bag around a terrifying foreign airport and into the terrifying foreign airport lavatory where you have to rest it on your knees, because the floor is completely out of the question. Meanwhile all those people foolish enough to stow their luggage are strolling about stretching luxuriously and doing some more airport shopping.

The final insult comes when you reach your pensione and find that everything in the stupid carry-on bag is crushed beyond recognition and covered in a layer of Beauty Flash Balm. Marvellous. It's the only way to travel. Can't imagine why anyone would ever check their bags.

See you at carousel three.

Learning from the lovable eccentrics

Is international style guru Anna Piaggi stark raving mad, or has she figured out a brilliant solution to the fashion problem? Look, here she comes just a-walking down the street in velveteen pantaloons, an admiral's coat, a miniature top hat and a *ruff* that wouldn't look out of place on Sir Walter Raleigh. And that's just daywear. We won't even get into the blue-streaked and shaved hair, or the boiled lolly rings on every finger. The chick is crazy. Kooked. Flip city.

But although she dresses like she's on day release from the high security wing, Planet Nuts, Piaggi — who once came to Sydney for Australian Fashion Week with her usual container load of nuns' nighties, laughing cavalier hats and velveteen straitjackets — is worshipped in high fashion circles.

She works for the Bible (Italian *Vogue*). She's Karl Lagerfeld's great friend. She's front row à-go-go at every fashion show from Faubourg St Honoré to 7th Avenue. Calvin, Romeo and Helmut are always thrilled to see her, and I admit I was one of those out at the Sydney fashion shows mouthing *Isn't She Marvellous?* every time she turned up there looking like a troll doll on acid.

But I don't think she's quite as loopy as she looks. I reckon what Piaggi must have figured out, sometime in the early 1960s, is that you can jump off the fashion treadmill, even when you are one of the donkeys which turn it, by becoming a Lovable Eccentric, one of those wild and wacky individuals who wear whatever they feel like, completely untrammelled by trend and convention.

You know the people I mean. They look wacko the diddlyo and they don't care; in fact, they love it. Their style might be defined by a colour (usually purple), or a bygone era, like the freeze-framed folk who carry on dressing as they did when they were young and beautiful (Princess Margaret), or from a time they wish they'd lived in ('punks' born after 1960).

The 1950s is a favourite togzone for these types. Witness the Sydney-based lipstick entrepreneur who always dresses like she's off for a clam bake with Elvis, her denims rolled up to the calf, her hair in a bleached blonde quiff. And then there are those twits in London who get around in the full Edwardian Monty all the time. Even on Saturday mornings.

Op shop treasures we mere normals would not have been able to distinguish from the general tangle of stained polyester and free-form acrylic knits feature large on the lovably eccentric shopping list, along with kaftans, beads and all manner of ethnic tat.

This is clever, because it makes getting dressed very cheap. You can get a look without getting a loan. Anna Piaggi practically emptied an Oxford Street Javanese scarf shop while she was in Sydney, scoring a trunkful of new geegaws for the price of one Jil Sander trouser leg. And once you are outside fashion in this way, it must be such a relief never to be confronted with the moment when your favourite $900 jacket stops whispering 'last season' and starts yelling TWO YEARS AND HOLDING.

Plus, as a lovable eccentric, you need never worry about being inappropriately dressed, because you always will be – by other people's cramped suburban standards, that is. By your own, you will never look anything short of mag-nificent. Look at me, see me shine in my patchwork satin shortie jelabah, my rainbow head wrap and my favourite emerald-green Doc Martens.

The truly fashion-enslaved suffer for their obsession, but lovable eccentrics just have a heap of fun with the whole thing. While you and I are wondering whether we can wear velvet in December, or a straw hat to the autumn racing carnival, they are bum up in the dress-up box rootling around for their favourite purple cloak. Now who looks stupid?

Fat chance

I like Lycra. Lycra likes me. Lycra and I are in such harmony that every time I breathe in, Lycra breathes in and, more importantly, every time I breathe out, Lycra breathes out. Let it go. Aaaaaaaaah.

Lycra is my friend. Lycra makes me feel like I'm wearing pyjamas when I look like I'm wearing tailored pants. With Lycra you can get off a plane looking like you mean business, feeling like you're wearing a tracksuit. Lycra is so comfy that, if you close your eyes when you are wearing trousers, a skirt or even a whole suit containing it, you feel as if you're in one of those dreams when you've gone to work in your nightie.

Lycra makes dressing so easy. They put it through everything these days. Remember when it was just in shiny gym gear? Spandex – ha! Now it's in every fabric, from simple cotton drill to satin and the most expensive wools. You can even get a raincoat with Lycra in it, if you really want one.

It's used in underwear, so knickers don't sag, and in body shirts, so they cling. It's used in tight tailored jackets that feel like cardigans and in crêpe evening dresses that fit where they hit and drape where they don't.

And there's more. It resists creasing. Garments worn day after day hold their shape. It adds clingy zing to the simplest garment. Lycra is freedom. Lycra is glamour. Lycra is one of the greatest inventions of the twentieth century.

But.

Butt. Butt and gut. Like many good friends, Lycra doesn't always tell you the hurtful truth. A pair of Lycra pants worn several times a week will accommodate a slowly expanding waistline with no protest. As your girth steadily increases, your friendly trousers ease ever outwards. On they go, every morning, and you think, 'How marvellous. I got married in these trousers and they still fit me.'

The problem is that your Lycra pants have middle-age spread, too. Not only do they wax and wane with the natural monthly cycle of a woman's womby area, they are also capable of sustained growth.

Over the months, a pair of Lycra pants gradually grows. It's a very slow process, like the formation of a stalactite, but after a couple of years of constant wear and not enough sit-ups on your part, a size-ten trouser will have swelled beyond a twelve.

The real problem is that you don't realise what has

happened until you blithely try to slip into a pair of trousers you used to wear before you discovered Lycra. They'll feel like a tourniquet. These are tough-love trousers which aren't afraid to tell you the truth. Fatty.

So take heed. Enjoy the cosy comfort of Lycra but, like all things, use it in moderation. Every now and again remind yourself what it is like to wear real clothes. Clothes that don't take into account that you have to eat a lot of big lunches for work, or that you can't bear to throw away the food the children leave.

And do the odd sit-up.

Lycra makes me feel like I'm wearing PYJAMAS when I'm wearing TAILORED PANTS

$\mathcal{T}een \quad queens$

This is one for the girls. Teenage girls. I have been spending a lot of time in the company of this species of late, with my own four nieces and some friends' daughters. Really, it would be hard to meet anyone nicer.

They are very funny and they sure can cuss good. They are still young enough to be enthusiastic and cuddly and to find wrinklies interesting (if a little stupid).

They like all the good stuff. Clothes, boys, shoes, make-up, pizza, *King of the Hill*, soccer, Charlotte Brontë, Matt Le Blanc, Joni Mitchell. And if you win their trust, they will even get their old Barbies out from under their beds and let you play with them.

There is nothing they like more than spending a glorious sunny afternoon watching *Roman Holiday* on cable with the curtains closed and a never-ending packet of Tim Tams. Plus they care deeply about wogongs, global warming and stray dogs. They oversee the household recycling and do sponsored swims for breast cancer research. They hate the Spice Girls. You see, superior beings.

Which is why I am concerned that they are not being fully educated in some of the little details that will make adulthood more congenial. So here is my list of:

Things I wish I had known at 14

Washing-up liquid applied directly to the fabric can remove most known stains.

Never wear a hat wider than your shoulders.

Never wear white to a wedding, as you may upstage the bride.

Never shave your legs – learn to wax your own.

Wearing scent before noon is inconsiderate.

Too much mascara makes you look cheap – learn to dye your own eyelashes.

Braces on your teeth are worth it, as are sensible shoes, at least until you stop growing.

Only people with very beautiful hands and very beautiful rings can get away with jewellery on their forefingers.

Don't let anyone cut your cuticles, ever.

Make the most of fun, cheap clothes, as this is the last time you will be able to wear them.

Stick-on tattoos are a laugh; real tattoos are a liability.

Send a written reply to wedding invitations.

Expensive drycleaners are worth it, but you can hand-wash a lot of things which say Dry Clean Only.

The girl at school who gets kissed the most now may not be happy in later life.

There is no such thing as nice cheap shoes (except espadrilles).

Don't believe everything you read in magazines.

White shoes, white handbag – don't do it.

Your mother is right when she says your physics homework is more important than watching *The Simpsons*.

Likewise when she says your hair needs a trim.

There are other hairstyles apart from the centre parting.

At a formal dinner or luncheon with place cards, turn yours around so other people will remember your name.

Those cheap wash-out hair dyes from pharmacies are probably not as nice as your own hair colour.

Work hard at French.

It is never too early to establish a skincare routine.

On Friday nights you can dress as trashily as you like (but you don't have to behave that way too).

Thankyou notes will get you everywhere.

You are young and you are gorgeous.

Use sunblock and you'll stay that way.

You do not need to go on a diet.

The virus

I think I've got a virus. There's a really nasty 24-hour bug going around and I think I've got it. Everyone's had it. The symptoms are a splitting headache, strong waves of nausea, a very dry mouth and an intense craving for bacon and eggs. I've got them all.

It must be one of those mutant resistant strains, because it keeps going away and then coming back. Some of my friends have had it several times. You think you're over it, then you wake up and have it all over again. The only thing that seems to make it better is Coca-Cola. I've really got a bad dose this morning.

It's not just physical, either, this virus. It gives you these intense feelings of self-hatred and some of the great unanswerable questions of life go around in your head like a toy train. Why did I do chew and show in Rockpool? Why did I decide to start drinking Cointreau at 2 am? Why did I do a pole-dancing display with a lamppost in Devonshire

Street? Why did I sing 'Good Year for the Roses' using a beer bottle as a microphone?

Another symptom is unexplained bruising all over your body, especially on your back. I've got a corker on my left buttock. Roughly the same shape as Taiwan and about the same size.

Come to think of it, maybe it's not a virus. Maybe I was mugged, because there was $200 in my wallet last night and there's only a five this morning. And where did those Star City matches come from? I don't smoke and there's half a packet of Marlboro Lights in my bag. I was mugged and they put cigarettes in my handbag to confuse me.

I think they left their phone number, too, because there's something that looks like the word Simon and a Paddington number written on a beer mat. In eyeliner pencil.

And why do I have an Amex receipt for $154 which seems to say 'Bourbon and Beefsteak' on it? I don't even like bourbon. Don't think about whisky. Don't think about whisky.

I'm going to vomit.

Maybe if I have another sleep I'll feel better. I can't sleep, the bed is full of crumbs. I'm too hot. I'm too cold. I'm going to clean my teeth. God, this toothpaste is rough.

I must have food.

I've had four pieces of toast and Vegemite, a tomato, a black banana and some Sara Lee ice-cream. It was all we had, but it's not enough. I've got to have eggs. Maybe I'm pregnant. I feel nauseous and I've got food cravings.

I'm getting up. I'm going to Victoria Street, if I can make it up the hill. Fried eggs. Crispy bacon. Toast dripping with butter. Butter dripping with butter. Orange juice. Tim Tams. Coca-Cola. Chocolate ice-cream. Chocolate Paddle-pops. Caramello Koalas. Maybe I'll get a taxi to Woolloomooloo and have a pie. Maybe I'll get a taxi to the bathroom.

I'll tell you another thing about this virus. It really puts you off alcohol.

Smart casual

There are two words which strike terror into the wardrobes of even the most confident of stylemeisters: Smart Casual.

This is a clothing concept which makes otherwise sensible people do things as foolish as tucking the back of their polo shirt in while leaving the front hanging out, or wearing sandshoes without socks. Just two examples which make it quite clear — it ain't smart and it ain't casual.

No other dress code instils such anxiety. An embassy ball in Paris? Not a problem. Lunch with Nan Kempner at Le Cirque? A cinch. Highland dancing at Balmoral? I'll press my plaid. But a barbecue in Toorak — *forget* it, I haven't got a THING to wear.

One prominent Australian fashion commentator, who dresses for the Melbourne Cup and Paris fashion shows with effortless chic, told me recently she has come up with the perfect solution for smart casual dressing — she doesn't go out at weekends.

I think she's on to something. I'd certainly be happier throwing a quick look together for Truman Capote's Black and White Ball than for an afternoon watching polo at Warwick Farm.

But why, you may well ask, does it matter a jot what you wear to sit on a piece of parched grass in a semi-industrial area of Sydney and watch sweaty men thundering up and down on sweatier horses?

Well, it doesn't really (unless you are harbouring ambitions to help an Argentinian get the stains out of his britches after the last chukka); but, semiotically speaking, what you wear to tread the divots matters hugely.

Because to get smart casual wrong, to be overdressed at the polo, high-heeled on a Halverson, or absolutely unkempt at absolute waterfront Sunday morning drinks, is to reveal yourself as hopelessly unsophisticated. Smart casual is an international secret society and you're not a member. Well, not in those denims and trainers, sweetheart.

What makes it so hard is that, unlike the cast-in-stone traditional commandments of short for cocktails, long for white tie, these are unwritten rules. The coded laws of smart casual make the Dead Sea scrolls look as straightforward as the Kings Cross Coca-Cola sign.

And it's all too easy to be a smart casualty. There are so many cringey little traps to fall into. Too many red accents, too much mixing and matching, and you'll just look *jaunty*. Stripes and anchor prints? Natty. Cheap old clothes meticulously starched and ironed? Band-box smart.

If you don't get it just right you can be accidentally feral (T-shirts with attitude problems) or Gold Coast (white denim, gold shoes, belts, baseball caps and teeth). Or just look like you live in Mosman, or Malvern (ironed jeans).

But, in fact, the secret of successful smart casual is very simple. All you need to do is buy some ridiculously over-priced clothes, called 'Designer Sportswear' (which just means paying fifty times the Target rate for some cotton jersey), and then treat them with utter contempt.

Why, these white pants only cost me $300, of course I don't mind sitting on wet grass/in the ocean spray/next to the barbecue in them. To get comfortable with that feeling, wear them first to clean the hull of your boat, or to re-grout the bathroom. Put them in the dog's basket straight from the carrier bag.

As long as the clothes scream Expensive, your demeanour screams Like I Give A Shit and your mouth screams Hello Darling!, you'll be part of the casually smart set.

Or you could just stay in.

Why men hate pantaloons

Men don't like women in culottes. They also loathe knickerbockers, pantaloons and, unless they are on a belly dancer, harem pants.

Perhaps it's not surprising that men dislike these particular garments – they are silly, contrived novelty items that women hate, too. Well, we hate them most of the time, except when fashion designers get desperate for a new idea and put them up on a catwalk. Then we realise we've loved them all along. And six months later we run with them to a clothing bin. At night. In false beards.

All it takes is for Karl Lagerfeld to put, say, jodhpurs in a Chanel show and in a few months' time we'll all be wanting a pair. They wouldn't even have to be sexy, form-fitting, showjumper jodhpurs – we'd even embrace big balloony Cecil B. de Mille jodhpurs if they style them right.

And men will be wondering all over again why we can't stop wasting money and just wear leather miniskirts and high heels all the time.

It's not just jodhpurs and baggy trousers and leggings that men detest. They don't really like any of the clothes women wear. They're suspicious of any kind of geometric print because they remind them of caravan holidays and aunties. Any loud design or over-fussy details make them nervous.

They're not wild about the opaque tights that all women love because we think they make our legs look thin. Men think they make us look like Greek widows. And they absolutely detest those stretch leggings which we think make us look streamlined in comfort.

If we're really honest, men don't really like any form of trouser on a woman, apart from the right jeans on the right girl, or hipsters on anyone with a flat brown stomach. And they hate them for the same reason they hate culottes. Access. Lack of.

It's a conceptual thing rather than a practical consideration. We're not suggesting that men really expect instant access to women's crotchular regions at all times. But they sure like thinking about it. That is why they particulary hate culottes. A woman bowling along in culottes looks as if she's wearing a skirt. Then you realise she is wearing culottes. An unskirt. It doubles the insult.

Possibly the only thing worse is a new invention from

America which even has a horrible name — a 'skort'. This is a pair of shorts with a skirt flap over the front of it. My thirteen-year-old niece thinks they're great for hanging upside down on the jungle gym, but her thirteen-year-old boy pals already know they should hate them.

So what do men like? They like dresses and they like skirts (which they call dresses). Generally, short skirts, although long wafty skirts are sometimes acceptable. Especially if they have a tendency to cling or become see-through with the light behind them. But most of all they like short skirts and bare legs.

Not that we care. Women dress for each other, anyway. You should see my new jodhpurs.

Swimwear and tear

Now is the time for all good women to go and buy swim-suits. Good morning and welcome to hell.

I have it on good authority that even women with great bodies hate buying swimmers. They are such small objects that even a millimetre of fabric here, and not there, can make the difference between Pamela Anderson and Pam Ayres. And although they be ever so small, they are very important and meaningful garments, because each swim-suit defines a summer.

Yet consider the circumstances in which we are forced to buy them. Go swimwear shopping in some groovy surf-side bikini-tique and you will be expected to strip off behind a flimsy curtain and then walk into the *centre of the shop* to look in the mirror. Who came up with that one? Dr No?

Look for swimsuit sanctuary at the other end of the mar-ket and you will find that our best department stores have special changing rooms for trying on 'resort wear' (which actually means overpriced swimsuits). These cubicles are known in the trade as 'torture chambers'.

The first thing you will notice about these Room 101s (apart from the fact they make you immediately want to go to the toilet) is the lighting. I know it is oafish and cheap to look tanned these days, but I don't want to look like something from the Sydney Fish Markets either. Perhaps I'll ring up Tetsuya and see if he has any witty ideas for my thighs. He could use them instead of abalone in a wobbly little entree.

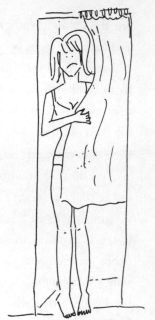

You will be expected to walk into the CENTRE OF THE SHOP to look in the mirror

Then there are the helpful assistants who barge in unannounced just as your arms are pinioned like Houdini by an impossibly small piece of Lycra that you can't get on and you certainly can't get off. This is a bikini. That red thing coming out of the top of it is your face. That thing coming out of the bottom of it is your body. Hello, gorgeous, want to come to my yacht for a dry martini?

But the really unforgettable feature of the torture chambers are the cunningly angled mirrors to show you exactly what you look like from behind in your potential new bathers.

Watch my hips: I do not want to know what I look like from behind in a swimsuit. If I knew the truth about my rear view I would have to walk backwards into the water for the rest of my life. Which is out of the question, because then everyone on the beach would see my front.

And don't come out with that old 'No-one will be looking at you . . .' line. I've been hearing it my whole life from my mother and I know it's not true on the beach. Because there is nothing more fascinating than looking at all the other women and comparing them with yourself. This is why I've never understood the concept of a great book for the beach. I'm always too busy checking out the chicks.

Then, if you're *sur la plage* for a relaxing day with your partner, you can quickly drive him insane asking questions like this:

'Am I as fat as her?'

'Which woman on this beach do you think has the best figure?'

'Which woman on this beach has a body most similar to mine?'

Which will take both of your minds off the fact that he is lying there quite happily, with his hirsute stomach standing proud of baggy ten-year-old laddered Speedos. And absolutely no idea what he looks like from behind.

Tied to the
clothes rails

I can't believe I'm back to clothes rails. I thought that like trainer wheels, cider and Eurorail, they were something you grew out of – as in over, not likely, never again.

Yet here I am once more with my all clothes on wobbly racks, covered in Balinese sarongs in a hope it will protect them from moth maggots and make them look kind of arty and bohemian. As opposed to just plain tragic. Welcome to my bedsit.

I feel like such an amateur. Rolling clothes rails from K-Mart, while functional, if not downright indispensable during the student and first job stage of life, are like a provisional licence, before you get to drive the built-in wardrobe and, ultimately, the Volvo Estate of clothes storage – the walk-in closet.

Actually, I am writing this in a walk-in closet. Only

normally it would be called a 'spare room used as study'. Sure there is a desk, a computer, a printer, a fax, lots of unopened bank statements and other officey things, but there are also three clothes rails and a wall of stacking wire storage baskets which looks like London Transport's lost property depot.

It's not a conceptual art installation called The Randomness of Umbrellas Part II. This is my new home. Because I have accidentally moved into an apartment with no cupboards.

When I say none, I mean there are cupboards in the kitchen and one long, thin one in the bathroom, which would be good for hanging salami, but nothing where you could put a spare handbag or twelve, your collection of souvenir scarves, or forty pairs of shoes. Not even a shelf for bangles, or a hook for a baseball cap. But, hey, I shouldn't complain. There are plenty of doorknobs to hang beads on. And I'm lucky – I've *got* clothes rails. I could have all my clothes hanging from the curtain rails on wire hangers.

I didn't do it on purpose; I didn't choose a unit with less storage space than a Formula One car for the challenge. It was just that I was so in love with the cleanness of the bathroom and the treeness of the view that I didn't notice the notness of the cupboards until after I had signed the lease.

But there is one thing that makes me less unhappy about the prospect of all future visitors sleeping on the sofa (and as I seem to be regressing to age twenty-two, they will probably bring their own sleeping bags): at least there are no clothes and shoes in my bedroom.

I grew up in a house where the major bedrooms had dressing rooms, and I still think it is rather vile to sleep amid smokey jackets and warm shoes. We didn't have dressing rooms because we were disgustingly rich, I should point out. The house had them because it was old — Georgian houses had dressing rooms because they had to have somewhere to keep their wigs. After that we moved to a Victorian house which had a 'box room', because they had to have somewhere to keep their trunks and Gladstone bags. Wasn't that sensible?

Now we buy more clothes in a month than a Georgian gentleman farmer or a Victorian explorer would own in a lifetime, and yet people are allowed to build units without so much as an airing cupboard, let alone a wig room. And lady journalists are forced to compose prose in the linen press. A pox on't.

Princess ballerina

Sophie is wearing her pink ballet leotard and matching cardigan, a net tutu specially stitched by House of Grandma, birthday wings from a fairy shop and a piece of old glittery advent calender as a head ornament. This is daywear.

She's playing with her favourite doll, Lady Samantha (actually a small plastic horse with a luxuriant pink nylon mane), who is wearing an equine wedding dress. Sophie is in the process of creating a four-poster bed for Lady Samantha from an old chiffon scarf, several coloured pencils and Blu-Tack. Going into her bedroom barefoot is very unwise at the moment, as tiny hard plastic hairbrushes, earrings and crowns belonging to this horse are likely to become embedded in your feet.

Sophie is four and going through the Princess Ballerina phase of female childhood development. At this stage, no matter how many agnès b. enfant black cardigans – just like Mummy's! — or organic cotton whale-print T-shirts — just like Daddy's! — are dangled in front of her, Sophie will dress only in pink Lycra and net. She spits on natural fibres. They don't sparkle.

Where does it come from? asks her mother, a tax lawyer, who bought Sophie a carpentry set for her fourth birthday, causing an emotional outburst so extreme she was forced to exchange it for a pair of play high heels and a pink plastic Keepers Kastle.

Mum's fantasy garments are a grey flannel Ralph Lauren pants-suit with concealed buttons and a pair of black patent J.P. Tod's. Sophie's are a fuschia lurex one-shoulder gown with satin frills and a concealed crinoline, and a pair of matching stiletto mules with fluffy pompoms. She's recently drawn this ensemble with fluorescent felt-tips and attached it to the fridge with a *Barbie* magazine fridge magnet (she's a subscriber).

'That girl,' says Mummy's special friend Colin, the one who smokes long cigarettes and lets Sophie have a look at his nipple rings, 'that girl is camper than Lily Savage.' With memories of his own fourth birthday still vivid (he tried to make high heels out of the Meccano and was severely punished), he bought her a tiara for her birthday. Sophie *loves* Colin.

'Mummy, when can I have nipple rings, diamond ones? And I want to have my ears pierced, like Colin's, Mummy, please can I, please?' says Sophie.

Somehow Freud omitted the Princess Ballerina stage from his model of human emotional development, but it is just as clearly defined as the oral and anal phases and just as crucial for a normal transition into adult clothing choices. Parents who attempt to suppress the natural expression of the phase with compulsory tasteful wooden toys, or non-pastel clothing, risk permanently damaging their child's taste. Deprive the girl of pink Lycra and she will wear it for life.

If left to act it out naturally, most young girls emerge spontaneously around eight years old, with a sudden burning desire to wear black polo necks and have sailing lessons, but fully grown women who never consolidated this stage — Barbara Cartland, Anna Nicole Smith, Baby Spice, etc. — are compelled to act it out for the rest of their lives. The predominant symptoms are a continued obsession with the colour pink, a large collection of cuddly toys and a love of fluffy white dogs. In extreme cases, they call their husbands or lovers 'Daddy'.

Sophie's mother agrees that allowing her child access to sexually stereotyped dolls with abnormally large breasts is better than that fate. Looks like Sophie's dead-set for Barbie's Dream Home, next birthday.

Fash mag slag off

I hate my life. I'm so ugly. I have no clothes. My home looks like the Ikea sale area. I used to think my ankles were slim and now I realise they are chunky. All my shoes are horrible.

I am so fat. I want everything. In every colour. I want to go everywhere. It's not fair, why can't I have a beach house on St Barts? Why aren't all my friends film stars? I feel so left out.

I don't normally feel like this, but I've just read a fashion magazine. If it's a good fashion magazine that is how it makes you feel. The worse you feel, the better you know the magazine is. I spent a blissful hour this afternoon lying on the sofa looking at British *Vogue* and now I feel like the Elephant Man's less attractive sister. Except even she has better clothes than me.

What a great magazine it is. It has made me feel so bad. Exquisite torture, that is what the glossies offer us every month. I've never been able to get enough of it myself.

This the the way it works. Every time you read a fashion magazine you realise you won't be allowed to join the groovy gang unless you lose twenty-five kilos, buy an entirely new wardrobe, get a famous husband and property on Long Island. And by the time you get back with the carrier bags, the engagement ring and the title deeds they will have compiled a new 'out' list with everything you've just bought on it.

'Southampton OUT South Carolina IN,' it will say.

What is the area code for Charleston anyway?

The funny thing is that even if you have all the kit, I'm not sure that anyone is actually a member of the fash mag club. I've edited two of them myself and even then I didn't feel like a member. And I knew it was all lies.

Well, it's not all lies. When they say that rubbing a very expensive petroleum-based goo into your face will make you look like Elizabeth Hurley, that's all true of course. And it's also true that you can't possibly get through to next spring without buying six new pairs of shoes and one of the new Fendi handbags. That's gospel.

Where the lying comes in is the impression glossy mags give that there are people somewhere – somewhere you are never going to be invited because your legs are too short and you can't do smart casual – who really lead the perfect lives they appear to lead in fashion magazines.

You know the place: a heavenly house full of unique

little touches, darling children with French haircuts, simple yet elegant food with an original twist, a couple beaming contentedly at each other over the home-made quince paste, surrounded by glamorous friends, feeling completely relaxed.

Nobody's waistband feeling a little tight.

This place doesn't exist. Some people are pretty fabulous, but nobody is totally completely utterly fabulous, the way they appear in fashion magazines. It just isn't possible.

I've seen people I know featured in glossy mags sharing their recipes for green tea salad and radish risotto with all of the rest of us sad drongos, as they entertain fifteen of their effortlessly chic friends in their perfect weekender.

I nearly fell off the sofa laughing. I know these people; they are hopelessly neurotic sods who spend the whole weekend drunk or hungover, and having sex with inappropriate people. (That's why I like them, actually.)

But even though I knew that particular story was total codswallop ('Briony likes to grow rare species of Belgian lettuce and Robert has a large collection of antique watering cans picked up at garage sales and swap meets'), it didn't stop me from being completely taken in by every other story in the mag. I knew my friends were frauds, but everyone else in there was perfect.

They must be, they were in a glossy magazine.

The secret language
of handbags

Your handbag is not a silent partner. Wherever you go it is speaking volumes about you. You may think it's just a bit of dead cow hanging off your shoulder when actually, it's like a personal Reuters screen, broadcasting exactly how highly you value your personal stock.

If it's a neat leather shoulder bag which complements your general attire and can still remember the last time a soft cloth was passed over it, your SP (Selling Price) is pretty high. Likewise if it's a classic bag, old and worn in, but clearly loved and looked after. But if it's a scuffed and sagging satchel, with a broken fastening, a fraying strap and things falling out of the sides, your Reuters screen is flashing SELL SELL.

The reason handbags are such articulate self-signifiers is that they are the whole of our lives in microcosm. The stuff in your handbag is what you feel you cannot get through the day without. It's an instant indicator of your priorities – and our priorities define us. Which is why that women's magazine classic, 'Five Famous Women Show What They Keep In Their Handbags', is always so gripping.

I know women (and they are not war photographers) who carry their passports in their handbags at all times; others who have enough photos to fill a family album; gals whose bags contain alarm clocks, a pharmacy, the David Jones cosmetics hall, an entire lolly shop, five paperbacks, dog biscuits in case they meet a hungry stray, rooting powder in case they want to pinch a plant cutting and all their bank statements. Other handbags are devoted variously to breath freshening, hairdo maintenance, family planning and in-flight entertainment. Some are tiny and contain only keys, credit card and a condom.

The contents of every handbag are as individual as the woman hauling it around. And as the state of the outside indicates how you feel about the stuff inside, are you really happy to carry your entire identity in a scruffy old sack?

Like all things sartorial, it's not just about money. A reasonably priced handbag that is properly looked after can do more for you than the latest Gucci classic, scratched and overfilled. One well-maintained designer bag for a lifetime is better than a faddish parade of the latest styles. Especially if it is a Kelly bag from Hermès.

These handmade handheld bags with the distinctive brass padlock closure (the tiny key hangs off the handle in a little leather slip cover, couldn't you just die?), as designed for Princess Grace of Monaco when she was still just Miss Grace Kelly, are the ultimate statement of handbag self-esteem. They are in such demand worldwide, you have to go on a waiting list for a black one. They cost upwards of $6500 each.

Yes, it's a ridiculous amount of money, but not all the women buying these bags are millionairesses. It is a rite of passage for young middle-class Parisiennes to save up for one, and to see a woman in her fifties carrying a Kelly she has had since she was twenty, and which she paid for herself, is to see someone who knows exactly where she is in the world.

Which is why I reckon we need to take that formula for buying engagement rings — which says that the man should spend the equivalent of three months' salary on it — and apply it to handbags. Perhaps something like four times the price of the last pair of shoes you bought. Or five times as much as you ever thought you could spend on a handbag.

Help me out here, guys, I need to find some serious justification for the fact that I spent $800 on one last week.

A small
(but perfectly formed)
history of bosoms

I'm so glad I wasn't young in the 1950s. Well, I would have liked some of the shoes and the little bags and cocktail hats, but I would have looked awful in the clothes. All those cinched waists and pointy bosoms are so not me. I found one of those circle-stitched bras in a market once and bought it for fun. When I tried it on I couldn't figure out where my breasts were meant to go in the nose cones.

I would have been a hopeless flapper as well. The dancing looks like a heap of fun, but I would have had to have worn one of those breast flatteners, which is a pretty depressing thought. Now, 1940s gear I do like. My mum looked great in her uniform and we're exactly the same shape, but world war is a high price to pay for flattering tailoring.

I've always considered crinolines an insult to woman-kind, but late-Edwardian gear I think really is my favourite. All those divine white voile dresses for floating around eating strawberry tarts. And the hats! Heaven. I've got all the equipment for a monobosom too, so I would have been laughing. Plus I could have been a suffragette and done something worthwhile with my life.

The early 60s would have been *moi*. I've always wanted a twist dress and I am loving all those kinky boots and minis and the marvellous hairdos, but it was all over so fast, the Nancy Sinatra era. And while I adored the late 60s and early 70s on other people, I know I was just never coltish enough to carry it off.

It was illegal to have a bust in the early 70s. That is why I so envy the young gels of today who wear their bra straps as part of their look with singlets. When I was fifteen, a visible bra strap was social death. You were meant to have two pert mosquito bites which didn't need any harnessing. More than a mouthful was a waste apparently. Well, for those of us with a couple of platefuls that was hard to take. It was so bad I once resorted to a stick-on bra. Taking it off was like having your breasts waxed, but to have that no-bra effect without that braless look, I thought it was worth it.

That's the way it is with bosoms. At any time half the female population is either flattening them or padding them in the name of fashion. Which is why some of the mosquito-bite clan started having foreign objects inserted in their bodies, to create just-add-water cleavages, while bouncing platefuls are having their breasts half sawn off to look more *sportif*. I don't think either of these options is a good idea, I really don't.

Okay, fine, if a Band-Aid is an adequate bra for you, or you can't reach the supermarket trolley for the blighters, I can see that you might be tempted to take drastic action. But if they're just a little bigger, or a little smaller, than you and Mr Armani would like, please learn to love them anyway.

All bosoms are marvellous. They're miraculous, they feed people. And as so many women these days don't have any choice about saying goodbye to a beloved breast, it seems cavalier to mess around with a perfectly healthy one just because it's not this season's model, don't you think?

Your breasts are not accessories. They are part of you, not separate objects to be reduced or added to like a plasticine model. Even if fashion designers and *Picture* magazine do seem to see them that way.

In the 1970s I hated my breasts. In the 1980s I flaunted them. And now we just live quietly together. Me and my boozies. We're old mates and I wouldn't have them any other way. And I don't give a flying Wonderbra whether they're in fashion or not.

Anarchy   in   the   UK

People often trivialise fashion as a silly subject not worthy of serious attention, but believe me, fashion can be very serious indeed. I have been taken into police custody and charged for making a fashion statement.

It was the summer of 1977. Me and my best friend Paula had left our squat and proceeded down Clapham High Street in a southerly direction to our favourite greasy spoon.

Heaped plates of chips, beans and fried eggs had just been put in front of us when two rozzers and a police-woman burst into Nick's Caff and said, 'You two, out.' I looked around for the Kray twins before realising they meant us. 'But we haven't eaten our breakfasts and we've paid for them . . .' didn't wash with what I now realise was the Fashion Police.

They bundled us into a waiting panda car and took us to the station. 'What are we supposed to have done?' I asked, wondering whether the entire squat was being busted because a lot of the people living in it happened to be from Northern Ireland.

Maybe it was the Anti-Nazi League marches we'd been on, those small incidents involving asking for child's fares on buses, or the enormous amount of amphetamines consumed by some of our friends.

It turned out to be our T-shirts.

'We've had complaints,' said WPC Poeface, 'about the offensive nature of your attire.'

The garments in question featured a print by an artist I now know as Tom of Finland, depicting two magnificently endowed cowboys who had accidentally forgotten to wear their trousers and underpants. Underneath the drawing was the scandalous dialogue, 'Been out much?' 'No, it's been pretty quiet.'

We'd bought them at Seditionaries, Vivienne Westwood and Malcolm McLaren's boutique in the King's Road, where we bought all the clothes we didn't make ourselves. We'd starved ourselves to have them. We'd actually begged money off tourists at Sloane Square station to buy them.

They were the *dernier cri*, especially teamed with our bondage trousers, monkey boots, leather jackets and studded belts. The news hadn't quite reached the quiet folk of Clapham.

So we were charged with offensive behaviour, had our T-shirts confiscated and were booked into Lavender Hill

Magistrates Court. 'I'll look forward to seeing you then, girls,' sneered PC Sleazy. 'You'll be in nice dresses with your hair all combed. I know you middle-class girls.'

Needless to say, when I stood in the dock a couple of weeks later, my hair had never been spikier, my lips had never been blacker and I'd put extra studs in my leathers.

I guess we were lucky with the magistrate. He listened patiently to my defence that what was on our T-shirts was art. Would we have been arrested for wearing shirts printed with a picture of Michelangelo's *David*, I asked him. You can see far more offensive things on the top shelf of any paper shop, I told him, and they are photographs, not drawings. He seemed to agree, sentencing us to just six months' good behaviour bond. He even let us have our shirts back as long as we promised not to wear them.

I've still got my Tom of Finland Cowboys T-shirt and you know what? It's worth a fortune. Clothes from Seditionaries – the early work of one of Britain's most creative designers, the epitome of punk rock style – are now regarded as cultural icons. In short, my T-shirt is recognised as a work of art. I could sell it at Sotheby's.

Well, God Save the Queen. Although, come to think of it, it's probably a good job I wasn't wearing that Seditionaries T-shirt, the one with a safety pin through her conk. We could have ended up in the Tower.

As good as it gets

Is it just me, or do other people sometimes refuse at the final fence of fabulousness too? I don't know what goes on in my head, but from time to time I put together a look that is so right, so buff, I just can't leave the house in it. Someone might see me.

Take my new party dress. It is such a sassy little thing. Completely sheer, bias-cut, hand-printed red silk georgette. Hot diggity dog, this dress has an M rating. It positively sulks if you don't take it out dancing on a Saturday night and then it refuses to go back on the hanger before dawn.

Then there are my new shoes (the ones I bought when I was looking for something sensible for work). Leopardskin stiletto sandals. And that's *furry* leopardskin, mind you. They are the Eartha Kitt of footwear. So sexy they growl.

You can imagine how they get on together, shoesies and dressy. They adore each other. Every time I close my boudoir door I'm convinced they're having a secret dance party in there. They probably sneak out while I'm at work and lie around on the sofa drinking Campari and listening to Peggy Lee. If I came home one day and found an ashtray full of lipstick-tipped cigarette butts I wouldn't be remotely surprised. In fact I'm sure I heard a stifled giggle as I put my key in the door the other night and caught a whiff of Mitsouko in the hall.

That dress and those shoes are made for each other, it's plain. But can I get of the house wearing them together? Can I heck. I'm too shy. The whole is so much greater than the sum of the parts I just don't feel up to it. My clothes are better looking than I am.

I've worn the shoes with a very plain black pants-suit and then felt sad that no-one could see how marvellous they are. I wanted people to cross Oxford Street just to be introduced to them. And I've worn the dress with plain black shoes which really weren't up to the gig, and I could tell by the end of the evening they weren't talking to each other. Red dress was hissing, How could you let me be seen in public with these frumpy old things? While black sandals were mumbling, After all we've done for you, all those long plane journeys when we let you put us back on at the other end without a struggle, all those endless shopping days when we slid on and off without protest and didn't pinch you once, all those business meetings where our open toes allowed you to feel a bit frisky on the sly and how do you thank us? Make us go out with a trollop of a dress . . .

I'll get them together one day, I promise. I am working on it. I've been practising at home. You know: standing up, sitting down, walking, just being normal in an outfit so fierce it gets invited to parties without me. I'm in training for a forthcoming trip to Melbourne when I'm hoping the freedom of being interstate will give me the confidence to go out looking as good as I possibly can.

If you promise not to look.

Clothes zones

You know how the world has time zones? Cities have clothes zones. In Sydney this becomes harshly apparent at the point where the Darling Harbour bridge vomits packs of tourists into Market Street at the junction with Sussex Street – in other words, *haute* CBD.

Suddenly, from being in tourist la-la land, where members of the male species feel they can wander freely without shirts and young women mill around in obscenely short shorts, they are in serious City territory. This is a work zone where men wear jackets and ties on the hottest days and women attempt to dress for success whatever the weather.

In this context, tourists in their dress-for-excess outfits, which are fine for watching waterski displays and eating fatty snacks, look grotesque. They have passed through too many clothes zones without a change. They have clothes lag.

It can happen to locals too. I've had clothes lag in Sydney

between a swim at Bondi and a coffee in Victoria Street; and in Melbourne, going straight from a chic inner-city lunch at Il Bacaro to a Brunswick Street fact-finding mission.

But the first time I remember experiencing serious clothes lag was one hot, stinky summer in New York City. I was staying in the funky downtown East Village and Cyndi Lauper's 'Time After Time' was the song floating out of every doorway, which should fix the era for you.

Remember how she used to dress? That was normal in the East Village that summer. If it was falling apart, didn't go together and didn't suit you, it was perfect. Especially if it was made from egg yolk yellow cotton jersey. In fact, Madonna's character from *Desperately Seeking Susan* (er, Susan?) would have looked nattily overdressed hanging out on the block where I was staying.

So I spent a morning tooling around 8th Street and 2nd Avenue looking at second-hand books and clothes, buying candles in a groovy spooky witch shop and gnawing on an organic tofu donut with a wheatgrass juice on the side. I was wearing old army shorts, a 1950s bowling shirt, foul sneakers and artfully 'uncombed' (it took hours), tousled hair. Look, at least I wasn't wearing a bit of plaited T-shirt around my head.

Then I remembered I wanted something from Macy's discreet wear department (that's what they call undies), so I jumped the subway a few stops uptown.

Nothing seemed out of place at Herald Square, where

there were enough weirdos and desperadoes around for me not to realise I had crossed two crucial clothes zones. It wasn't until the assistant at the knicker counter gave me a very hard look when I handed her my credit card that I realised she probably thought I'd stolen it.

For on that subway ride I had unwittingly gone from East Village grunge, right through Chelsea's chic downtown zone, to the Midtown business zone, where secretaries are forced to wear American Tan 20-denier pantyhose on the sweatiest days of summer. Shorts and old sneakers just didn't fit. In a distance you could walk, I had gone from hep-cat local to low-life alien.

I've experienced it the other way too, catching a cab from a meeting at the Estée Lauder company's office overlooking Central Park straight downtown and realising when I got there that my pale yellow Giorgio Armani jacket might as well have had 'Mug Me' stencilled on the back. No wonder they all ride around Manhattan in stretch limos. They need somewhere to change.

Basic black

I've got a new dress. It's not black!!! It's not even navy blue, which is just black with a suntan. My new dress is some kind of a light brown colour I don't even have a name for (okay, mushroom) and it's not plain either, my new dress. It's got a really pretty pattern on it, like swirling mauve gum leaves. And another thing it's not is jersey. So it's not black, it's not plain, it's not jersey and it doesn't have a collar. Those are all the things it isn't. What it is, is a miracle.

It's a miracle that I ever tried it on, a miracle that I even noticed it, because everything I buy is black jersey and when I enter a shop my eye automatically filters out all other figurations. But something about this flippy little dress just leaped out and said, Why not take me into the changing room and see what happens?

So I did and discovered that silky fabric cut on the bias is very flattering to a girl and that a round neck is a possibility as long as the garment goes in slightly at the waist. And I also discovered that wearing colours other than black makes you feel differently about yourself. It's high summer, the light is bright and beautiful and I realise I am sick of walking around looking like a Sicilian widow.

So now I am making a huge effort not to wear black all the time. In the effort to shift from film noir to techni-colour I have now also bought a heavenly cream chiffon bias-cut skirt embroidered with pale lilac flowers and a sil-very grey silk jersey V-neck top. They are gorgeous things and I have been caught standing by the hangers stroking them because it is so long since I have owned anything so, well, pretty.

They make me feel rather super when I wear them, too. You feel sort of light and flirty, and – whether it matters to you or not – I think colours other than black make heterosexual men look upon you more warmly. It may be because your flowery frock and pink cardigan remind them of their grannies, but they get a smiley look in their eyes, rather than the usual 'Is this warrior woman going to hunt me down and Bobbit me?' expression that all-black ensembles inspire.

I am on day five. There was a mishap yesterday because it rained and I had to wear rain shoes. Dark brown acid-jazz trainers don't look good with a flowery dress (unless you are twenty and live in Fitzroy or Newtown), so I did acci-dentally revert to an all-black pant and jersey shirt ensemble, but I'm back on the programme today.

But the problem is that, unless I do the dress option, I'm finding it really hard to keep both ends burning. The silver top doesn't really go with anything I own apart from black trousers and skirts, but I reckon as long as I keep light colours near my face, it's not cheating. However, the only thing I own that really goes with the cream chiffon skirt is a cream cardigan, and when I put that on this morning it had strange brown stains on it, so it had to be a black cardie. I'm so hot.

I did try working the silver top back with the cream (as we say in fashion hep-talk), but there was an incident with noodle soup at BBQ King earlier in the week and it is amazing how small splashes of chicken broth show up on pale grey silk jersey. And now the cream skirt has biro on it from when I was addressing thankyou letters in a cab and we stopped suddenly.

I couldn't help thinking that neither soup nor ink would have shown on a black top, or a black skirt.

Also there is the underwear issue. The cream chiffon skirt is completely, illegally, sheer, so I am now the proud owner of a 100 per cent nylon, flesh-coloured half-slip which is as glamorous as a plaster cast. And about as comfortable in hot weather.

Then there is VNL to consider. This stands for Visible Nipple Line. It's something to do with physics — the refraction of light? fractions? — but every topographical detail of the aureole stands out in perfect bas-relief through a white bra and top. I have tried on exactly the same bra and exactly the same top in black. Mosque modest. I don't get it and I don't like it.

And don't even start me on what colour shoes and hand-bag I am supposed to wear with a mushroom and mauve dress. I have just been going the usual black but it does rather detract from the summery look I am trying to achieve.

I'm beginning to think there were a lot of good reasons I used to wear head-to-toe black every day, and I hereby declare: Black Is The New Black.

For the love of sewing

You know how food is love? I think sewing is love too. To make something for someone, with your own hands, whether it is a cake or a cape, is to spend all the time it takes to make it thinking about them.

When I was a kid most of my clothes were made for me by my mother, who actually hates sewing, so I knew it was a labour of love for her, or sometimes by my very giving big sister, who would make glorious things for me just because she felt like it.

Once she made me a pair of mauve and white gingham hot pants in two hours, so I could wear them to my first disco. She measured me in the school playground with her ruler and by 6.30 pm they were ready to go out dancing. She totally understood that in 1972 I could not go to that disco unless I was wearing hotpants.

Another day I came home and found her surrounded by skeins of glorious red and white mohair, with something wonderfully fluffy and stripey emerging from oversized wooden knitting needles. Who is that for? I asked. You, was the reply.

But the things that were most special to me were made by my gifted grandmother, who was a kind of *House of Eliott* dressmaker in London in the 1920s, making clothes for ladies in high society. She was seriously good at sewing. She did some of the fine embroidery on the Queen Mother's wedding dress.

My mother still remembers going with her to the House of Lords as a very small girl, when granny had fittings with Mrs Keppel, great-grandmother of Camilla Parker Bowles. The butler would bring her a glass of milk and a piece of fruit cake and she would sit very quietly on a stool watching the dress come to life beneath my grandmother's fingers.

On one occasion there was great debate about where a beaded panel should sit on a draped crepe evening gown. At waist level, or just below? Or perhaps just beneath the bust? My mother, age three, watched as it was pinned, unpinned, moved and pinned again, before piping up from her corner, 'On the side.'

Both women turned to look at her, looked back at each other and then tried it on the right hip. It was perfect. Peggy says she can still remember the look Mrs Keppel gave her.

Many years later when I stood fidgeting on a chair as Granny pinned a hem on something for me, I didn't realise quite what skilfull hands I was in, but I did know Granny could make anything.

I knew that she could take three patterns out of the big sewing cupboard and turn them into one unique garment. A collar from one, a lapel from another, pockets from the third. I also knew that she could sew perfect buttonholes by hand and that she could take a piece of fabric that was slightly too small for the job and make the pattern fit on it. And she always had the nap going the right way.

But what I especially loved about Granny making things for me was that she always involved me in the process of choosing the pattern and the fabric and the trimmings, so that when it was finished the garment was really mine. I would spend hours on the floor with the button box choosing the buttons while she cut and pinned and tacked and hemmed.

One outfit I particularly remember was a tailored culottes dress she made me when I was about seven. I chose a dark purple wool crepe and Granny suggested it would look nice with a contrasting braid to edge it. What colour would I like? I knew straight away it had to be green and saw Granny smiling to herself as she said she thought that was a very good idea.

It wasn't until years later that it struck me why. Long after all those trips to Westminster with her tape measure and pins, she still remembered the suffragette colours very fondly.

Trainers stink

Trainers aren't comfortable. They're not. I've just fooled myself into buying a new pair and they're not comfortable. They are the right size, but somehow it seems to take more effort to lift my feet in them than it does in ordinary shoes. I feel like I'm wearing seven league boots but I'm going nowhere fast.

And talk about hot foot. It feels like I've been dipped into the La Brea tar pits and I've only had them on for two hours. And it's winter. I think there might be little elves stoking boilers in the soles. Talk about big foot. I'm tiny in the trotter department and these things are so big they look like I've forgotten to take them out of the box.

No wonder they call them cross trainers. I'm really bloody cross that I bought them.

And another thing. They are absolutely bloody hideous. They look like someone was fooling around with a bit of old rubber in a jaffle iron in their garage and made the resulting mess into a pair of shoes as a joke. Hang on – isn't that how Nikes were actually invented?

It wasn't a cheap joke either. These heavy, hot, hideous hoof covers cost me $129. What was I thinking of?

I was thinking of fashion, as usual. Because really really ugly trainers, the ones we all stopped wearing when tasteful Vans came into fashion a few years back, are all the go in London and New York right now.

I first noticed it as a trend when English friends, who are so fashionable they meet themselves coming back, turned up at my place wearing these dayglo split-level high-rise expresso bongo trainers on their feet. They were so ugly they glowed. Gee whiz, I thought, if Andrew and Vanessa are wearing them they must be groovy. They live in Notting Hill. Vanessa was wearing them with a *skirt*.

But the real obsession set in last October when I was in Paris and I met this woman of about fifty who was wearing them. She wasn't a bag lady trudging around in something she'd found in a rubbish tin, she was a fashion person (which is another kind of bag lady – hers was Prada, as a matter of fact). She looked so great, I vowed to copy her outfit immediately.

She was wearing a pair of pinstripe pants in a light-weight fabric, which I could see from twenty paces were from agnès b., a tunic-shaped stomach-covering chenille sweater with a stand-up neck and trainers which resembled the Pompidou Centre. She looked fantastic.

And what really appealed to me was that she also looked comfortable.

Comfort and fashion so rarely go hand in foot, that I am always ready to embrace an opportunity to look like a woman and walk like a man when it comes along. Even if it means wearing trainers that resemble prototypes for the latest Mazda.

I already had the pants, tick that box; I managed to find the perfect chenille sweater after a three-month search and then today I bought the trainers. They don't make me feel like a chic Parisienne, they make me feel like a troll.

I'm going to customise them, blacking out all the brand tags with a texta and then I'll try various species of sock, perhaps some inserts and heel lifts. Then, if they're still really uncomfortable, I suppose I can always wear them to the gym.

Stay young and hideous if you want to be loved

I love the fact that I hate what the Young are wearing. I've been hanging out at a bar frequented by hordes of eighteen-year-old backpackers recently (as you do) and I can't get over how hideous they look. As I heard myself remarking to another old person, 'Don't you remember when we were young, how beautiful all our friends were? Look at this lot. They look like they need a good wash.'

At the time I was serious. I could see how attractive all the girls would be if they just had a nice bob haircut and did their nails and wore some fitted clothes instead of army surplus trousers nine sizes too big, acrylic jumpers and ski hats. And toe rings with dirty toenails. Shudder. Haven't they heard of Revlon?

But later when I was watching the new Run-DMC video and marvelling at how awful all the beautiful young folk looked breakdancing in their baggy clothes and bobble hats I realised that was the whole point. If I didn't hate what people younger than me were wearing they wouldn't be doing their job right.

I first felt a flicker of the generation gap when that piercing thing was big. I thought it was disgusting. But I was thrilled to be Horrified of Hunters Hill, at last, because I was beginning to think there was nothing the Youth of Today could do to disgust an old punk rocker like me.

We were pretty vile in our day. My boyfriend pierced his nose with a darning needle in 1979. The difference between having a pierced nose then and now is that he had to take it out because it got us barred from every pub in Dundee. He practically got arrested. And in my King's Road days I had a friend who gloried in the name of Tampax, because she always had one hanging from a hole in her ear. (Unused; we weren't that disgusting.)

For a long time the generation younger than me didn't seem able to find their ugly feet. It was like they knew they had missed out on punk and couldn't top it. The post-punk gang were like the early 70s crew who didn't know what to do after the glory of the hippy thing. Until someone invented D-I-S-C-O and it all got interesting again.

Funnily enough, the first stuff I couldn't understand because I was too old was dance music also. It still thrills me how much I hate techno. I really don't get all that hero DJ stuff either. I thought they were people you hired to play records, now they seem to be stars in their own right. And why won't any of them play 'Car Wash'?

I knew Nirvana couldn't really be any good because I loved their music the first time I heard it. The Prodigy must be good though, because I absolutely hate them. Not with the total contempt I feel for the Spice Twits and anyone who buys their records, but with an awful fear that they represent the end of the world as I know it. I would hate one of my nieces to bring that awful Keith home.

The values expressed in the Prodigy's lyrics ('Smack My Bitch Up'? Charmed I'm sure, care for a lamington, Keith dear?) appal me the way the Sex Pistols appalled my parents, so they must be okay. I absolutely detest what Keith wears, I hate his stupid pointy hair and his yukky tongue. I don't think he's doing anything new and at least Sid Vicious was beautiful. Well, I thought he was. I thought he looked like a wasted poet in plastic trousers. My father thought he looked like a good candidate for target practice.

But then my ageing memory plays funny tricks. In my reveries, all my young cronies looked like people in a Ralph Lauren ad, or extras from *Brideshead Revisited*. Well, some of the time we did look like that. Most of the time we looked like rejects from a Run-DMC video.

Quality blondes

How many blondes does it take to change a light bulb?

How do you expect me to know? I'm a blonde.

Ha ha ha ha ha ha ha.

Although we all get branded with the same ignorant prejudices (see above), there is actually more than one kind of blonde. There is Pamela Anderson and her tarty tribe, there are brunettes in blonde bodies like me, and then there is another kind of blonde. More of your Diana Windsor than your Barbara Windsor.

She's the Quality Blonde, the kind of girl who makes a pair of jeans, flat J.P. Tod's shoes and a man's shirt look ineffably chic. She can sling a little knit around her shoulders without looking contrived. She can wear the tiniest slip dress with high heels without looking cheap. She always has a good watch and a good bag.

She usually has a rich boyfriend too. Not because she's a gold-digger – the QB usually has plenty of dough of her own – but because, like a Patek Philippe or a Maserati, a genuine QB is a luxury item, as rare as a champion race-horse and usually with as clear a picture of her bloodline.

It's incredibly annoying, but QBs just seem to come from the deep end of the gene pool. For centuries the richest blokes have married the prettiest gels and the result is an unbroken line of Quality Blondes traceable back to 1066. Many of the daughters of the great English houses have this look (that's the ones who aren't walking around in bobble hats and combat trousers . . .). Girls like Lady Helen Windsor and Lord Mountbatten's grand daughter India Hicks. They're blonde, they're rich, they make you sick.

But with Diana gone, the American Miller sisters, whose megabucks father owns the DFS duty-free shops around the world, are the reigning Quality Blondes of this era. Their blonde hair is always perfectly straight. The only thing straighter than their hair is their teeth. The only thing whiter than their teeth is their pearls. They all married princes, except the one who had to make do with a Getty, poor little love.

The other Queen QB *du jour* is Carolyn Bessette Kennedy, who married the closest thing America will ever have to Prince William. But before them all, there was Grace Kelly, the all-time Quality Blonde, another American who married a prince. In fact all Hitchcock's heroines were QBs. They were cool, but hell were they sexy. The QB has a chilly allure like diamonds and champagne, things they wear well and drink copiously. QBs never get pissed and throw up in the roses. They have good deportment.

Like I said, everything about Quality Blondes is annoying. You'll find them at polo matches and at grands prix, looking perfect in smart casual. Nobody does smart casual like a QB. That's why Ralph Lauren married one. In fact QBs find it easy to dress well in any style, because they are always very slim and have tiny ankles. They have trouble finding shoes narrow enough. They have skin which goes golden without burning and they never seem to need a leg wax. They have small pert breasts which are perfect for jumping on and off yachts in bikinis, but from which they can somehow produce a cleavage when they need one. Drives you mad. I think Quality Blondes are what made Christina Onassis's life so miserable.

Although you will find plenty of them at places where she used to hang out like St Moritz and Gstaad, QBs are not to be confused with their cousin the Chalet Girl Blonde, who is altogether a more robust and sturdy species, although both types wear chains on the same wrist as their Cartier watches. Camilla Parker Bowles is more your CGB. Her clothes never look quite right. Poor old Kanga was a CGB too, although Australia (particularly Adelaide) does produce its fair share of top QBs, always out in force at Flemington on Derby Day. QBs are very big on racing.

They look marvellous in hats and know instinctively how to walk so their heels don't sink into the turf.

Somebody once described me in print as a 'refrigerator blonde', which I secretly hoped meant the writer saw me as an ice maiden QB, although I never asked for fear he was thinking more of the American football quarterback nicknamed The Refrigerator, who wasn't blond at all. But actually I'm not sure I really want to be a QB. Like I said, they are so annoying, other women can't stand to be near them.

Oh, who do I think I'm kidding? Pass the peroxide, Pamela.

The cardigans

Good morning, Doctor, I know we've discussed it before, but I'm afraid I have more issues around packing. I know I've also brought up my problem with smart casual several times, but that's getting worse too. It gets really serious when the two are combined — as in Packing for a Weekend in the Country with Chic Friends.

I try to stay calm and remember that breathing technique you showed me, but really, what are you supposed to throw into your stylish little grip when you are going to one of those *Vogue Entertaining* houses where you know the salads will be better dressed than you?

Last weekend, as well as two pairs of boots, two pairs of suede shoes and one pair of sandals, I ended up taking five cardigans with me. I know this is not normal. I'm really worried that my cardigan fetish is getting out of hand, but they make me secure in a way no other garment can. Cotton, cashmere, silk jersey, short-sleeved, ribbed, hip-length with pockets; more like a T-shirt, more like a jacket, it makes no difference. I love them all.

I'm really worried my cardigan fetish is getting out of hand

When did I start to have these feelings? Well, the first garment I can remember deeply coveting on someone else was a pink angora bolero worn by the girl in front of me at my Year One Christmas carol singsong. I spent the whole of 'Once in Royal David's City' picking bits of fluff off it, until she noticed and told on me.

Actually, it started even earlier than that. My version of Linus's comfort blanket was a pea-green Granny-knitted V-necked cardigan. I took it everywhere. Why? To sniff, of course Doctor, what do you think I did with it? Wore it? You must be joking; even at three I knew that was an unbecoming colour. It wasn't a garment, it was my Sniffer.

My Sniffer was essential to the well-being of the whole family, and when I accidentally left it on a Spanish beach, my parents practically called in the SAS to help with the search. It was never found, but I soon replaced it with another home-knitted cardigan (speckled fawn, shawl collar, zip front) which I didn't lose. In fact, it went with me to university.

I never wore that one either. It was hideous. But mmmmmm, it smelled delicious.

I don't sniff my cardigans any more, but I do wear one most days to work. I usually have one to hand after six too, to sling round the shoulders of a little black dress. A cardigan and jeans is the only smart casual solution I've ever really been happy with. One of my favourite evening combos is a black cashmere cardie unbuttoned to reveal a hint of lace, with long skirt in a rich fabric.

And my neverfail gambit for those Martha Stewart country winter weekend fireside dinners is a navy-blue, long-line, man's cashmere cardigan, just sliding over a long jersey skirt, or pants. A red cashmere sock in a Gucci loafer and Nancy Cunard bangles complete the look.

Actually, that's not just any cardigan, Doctor. I inherited my navy cashmere cardigan, along with an identical one in grey, from my father when he died. He was a cardigan man of great distinction. Always cashmere and sometimes buttoned over a John Smedley cotton polo-neck, for a bit of a Roger Moore golf moment, but also to great effect after work, over a Brooks Brothers striped shirt and an Italian knitted silk tie.

Come to think of it, perhaps it isn't surprising that I associate cardigans with security, Doctor. You were right all along. They allow me to re-express childhood neediness and unresolved father issues.

And I thought it was because they were handy for keeping the draughts off.

Higher purchases

In just under two years Sydney will host the 2000 Olympics. Well, that will be lovely, I'm sure, especially if you fancy a T-shirt with an echidna on it. A much more significant event, as far as I am concerned, will be my Serious Shopping Silver Jubilee.

In July 2000 it will be twenty-five years since I first purchased a fashion garment solo. I'm going to print up some T-shirts asking 'Do you do refunds?' to celebrate the sunny day in 1975 when I walked into Miss Selfridge in Birmingham, England, and bought an item of clothing which I had chosen and saved up for all on my own. No parental presence or approval necessary.

We'll gloss over the fact that it was a short-sleeved, wide-legged denim jumpsuit. The point is that it was the first garment I owned entirely as a result of my own decision-making. I have been making bad decisions of this kind ever since.

But after a quarter of a century studying the science of retail therapy I have discovered that among the fake fur, the leg warmers and the fluoros, there are certain items that I will never regret buying.

Here I am happy to share with you my assiduously researched, elite group of perfect garments, shoes and accessories which never fail and, with any luck, will never change.

1. Bonds T-shirts

How do they get that cling without Lycra? The short raglan sleeves show off gym-plumped biceps to perfection. They look great under a business suit too.
Buy them: By the brace from all good gentlemen's outfitters.

2. The agnès b. V-neck cardigan with faggoting

I've never met a woman who owns just one of these. In fact, I recently met one who owns seventeen . . . Many have imitated, none have matched them. Flattering, comfortable and in different colours (especially black) every season, they are the essence of Paris in soft knitted cotton.
Buy them: Paris, London, New York, Melbourne (Daimaru).

3. The original shrink-to-fit Levi's 501s

Only these jeans are dark enough and you must sit in the bath in them to shrink them to fit, just like the advert. In

truth it is completely unnecessary, but it is the L-A-W.
Buy them: America. They just aren't the same anywhere else.

4. R.M.Williams boots

One piece of leather. A perfect boot. A miracle on your foot for the rest of your life.
Buy them: Australia.

5. Gap cotton 'crew' socks

Just thick enough, just thin enough, don't garrotte your ankles, cheap, great colours. They used to be a good enough reason in themselves to go to America — now we can get them here.
Buy them: Just about anywhere, including the Rocks and Sydney Airport International Terminal.

6. Suede sandshoes by Fila, style number 4EC507

A sandshoe which doesn't make you feel like a superannuated skateboarder. Wide enough for the more mature foot, chic enough to wear all the way from the East Village to the Upper East Side.
Buy them: I bought my black, navy and pale blue pairs at Office Shoes in London. Ask your local Fila stockist.

7. Black Saba sharkskin jackets

These are jackets you can tie around your waist at a rave

and wear to work the next morning. There's a subtly different cut and button configuration every season.
Buy them: Sydney, Melbourne, New York.

8. Gucci loafers

Not platform, not silver-snaffled, wannabe style, fake, or with socks — just the original Gucci snaffle loafer, in suede, for men and women.
Buy them: Duty free before you jet out, or Bond Street, Madison Avenue, Rodeo Drive, etc.

9. Hermès scarves

Jackie Onassis, Grace Kelly, Audrey Hepburn, that girl you've never forgotten in a St Germain cafe . . .
Buy them: As above, but so much nicer to buy at the main joint in rue Faubourg St Honoré in Paris.

10. House of Cashmere
100 per cent cashmere polo-necks

Not itchy, not too long, not too wide, not too tight, with arms the same length as yours. Not ridiculously expensive either.
Buy them: House of Cashmere, 12–14 O'Connell Street, Sydney (for other stockists, look up www.house-of-cashmere.com.au).

NB: It is quite permissible to buy all of the above in several colours. In fact, it would be rude not to.

Fancy this?

Well, the party season's over for another year. Did you have fun? Do you miss it?

I'm a bit sad I might not be slipping into my best little black dress for a while (bias-cut, shoestring straps, embroidered with flowers, practically dances the mambo on its own), but there are two things I won't miss: 1. Hangovers. 2. Dress themes.

I'm not talking about full-frontal Fancy Dress here, which can be the most fun in the world if everyone joins in, like the Cointreau Ball, but 'dress themes' for private parties which are much more vague.

When an otherwise chic invitation has a small line near RSVP saying something fey like, 'Dress: Disco Biscuit', or your host says, 'I thought it might be fun if everyone came as disco biscuits . . .' beware.

Because it can be mildly embarrassing if Birthday Boy has had the entire house rebuilt to resemble Studio 54 and raised Halston from the dead to design his outfit and you have just interpreted the 'theme' as a willingness to dance to 'YMCA' with arm movements, in your favourite Zimmerman frock.

But that kind of small faux pas is usually forgotten after the first chorus of 'It's Raining Men'. The other possibility is so much worse – and I speak from vile and terrible experience.

A 'friend' of mine once wound me and my (then) partner up into a frenzy of excitement with her plans to make her forthcoming birthday bash a 'Palm Springs party'. What a hoot it would be. We discussed the decorations and theme food for hours and several bottles of wine. She'd serve bowls of Miracle Whip, baskets of Wonderloaf, Ritz crackers with cream cheese from a tube, garnished with peanuts, and play Herb Albert and his Tijuana Brass all evening.

For a week, Geoff and I agonised over possible outfits before deciding to go as a cocaine dealer and his trashy girlfriend. I wore skin-tight denims with high heels, teased hair, frosted lipstick and false nails so long he had to come into the loo with me.

Geoff greased back his hair and slipped into a grotesque Hawaiian shirt under a white suit, with some white shoes he had found in an op shop, along with one of those hideous little men's handbags. He ran all the way home with it, he was so excited. He even grew an evil little moustache and practised sniffing, God bless him.

We were the only ones in costume. Phyllis had accidentally forgotten to mention the theme to anyone else and she was wearing an Azzedine Alaïa dress herself, I remember. Nobody talked to us all night. I felt like one of those albino crows which get pecked to death because they are feathered differently from the rest of the crowd.

But at least we had each other. My best friend Josephine was once invited to a garden gnome party. At least, she swears that is what they told her, but when she got to the barbecue in a belted yellow smock, with a pillow stuffed up it, scarlet leggings, Wellington boots, bright red cheeks, a Wee Willie Winkie hat, a white false beard and her brother's fishing rod, complete with rubber fish, there wasn't another garden gnome in sight. Not even a toadstool.

But being a game girl, and absolutely furious with her host (she had travelled to the venue on the London Underground), Josephine stayed resolutely in costume and character, dispensing gnomey wisdom and granting wishes with her magic fishing rod. You know what? She was the hit of the party.

The thrill of the till

Shopping for clothes has a lot in common with blood sports, mainly in that it is the chase (or, as they say in French, *la chasse*) rather than the kill that counts. Possession of the object of desire is not nearly as satisfying as the pursuit of it.

Just as huntsmen don't actually want to eat the fox, you don't necessarily intend to wear what you buy. You just want the fun of killing it. As Oscar Wilde might have said, shopping is the unspeakable in pursuit of the unwearable.

It's lovely going around lots of shops fingering all the really expensive fabrics. Trying on clothes you could never buy is thrilling. Especially if the shop assistants are snooty. It's like taking a Maserati for a test drive and then saying you won't take it, thank you, because you don't like the ashtrays. It's just the pockets on that Donna Karan suit you don't quite fancy.

A friend of mine once spent a whole afternoon trying on Chanel at Bergdorf Goodman in New York, inventing a new persona as someone about to marry a banker. John Galliano was making her wedding dress. Todd was on his way back to NYC on the Concorde.

She tried the lot on, with accessories, before sweeping off to a phantom lunch appointment having bought nothing. (She was wearing good underwear, so she knew she could get away with it.)

But fooling around aside, there is nothing like that moment when you decide, yes, that totally transparent $300 slip dress must be yours. Even though you know you will have to buy something specially to wear under it, or over it, to avoid arrest. Even though you will need new shoes, and possibly new legs, to set it off. Even though you'll have to have it altered and dyed a different colour, have your hair cut, lose five kilos and have liposuction to get away with it – you Must Have It.

It's not like you even went out looking for a slip dress. You were looking for saucepans. It doesn't make a gnat of difference that you've got three sheer slip dresses at home already, you haven't got this one.

The truth be told, you could probably make it right through to your seventy-fifth birthday without buying one more garment and never appear nude in public. But what you do need is to buy something, anything. *Now.*

It's probably a latent genetic urge that comes from our no longer having to scavenge for berries or track mammoths to stay alive that produces the irresistible need to shop. Some people ride around on horses in pursuit of an innocent furry mammal to satisfy this drive. Most of us head for the shops.

The moment of monetary exchange is triumphant (your spear has hit its mark, the mammoth is down), you beam as they wrap your conquest in tissue paper (they strap it onto a pole), and swinging down the avenue in a stiff paper carrier bag (toting it back to the cave) is pure bliss.

But wait until you get it home. Back in the reality of the pile of bills, the truthful mirror and the other three slip dresses, you are suddenly consumed with Post-Buying Depression. Your new dress is suddenly about as appealing as a bit of dismembered fox.

So put it away with the others and don't think about it. And next time you get the scent of blood in your nostrils, leave your credit cards at home.

Or only buy things you can eat.

The X-ray sex

Of course we grown-up girls don't dress for men. We dress for ourselves, to express our personalities, define our identities and boost our self-esteems. That is, the ten per cent of the time we are not dressing for men.

Oh come on, we *do*. Why else then am I so fond of this navy jersey shirt which showcases the bosomular area (discreetly, mind), while giving the cunning suggestion of a waist and artfully concealing any unwelcome activity in the stomachorial region?

Yes, it is also comforty and machine washable, but if I were really dressing for myself I'd be wearing pyjamas. Stretch pyjamas. With a kitten print. And fossil evidence that large groups of Vegemite toasts once lived in the area.

But the joke — as well as the flattering longer-line jacket — is on us. All men have X-ray vision. Not just Superman but any man can discern the exact shape of our bodies through all our beautiful tailoring and slenderising one-colour outfits. When you nip out for milk in that over-sized T-shirt and leggings, you might as well be naked. The long shirt over jeans manoeuvre? Gauze.

And just as they can see saddlebags through silk palazzo pants and spare tyres through tunic-over-stovepipe trouser combos, men can also spot insect waists and ice-cream scoop buttocks beneath mustard polyester.

Which is why some, well, *plain* women, with bad-hair lives and personalities as compelling as tofu are unaccountably popular with the chaps. Because underneath that made-in-India floral print viscose sack dress (the kind you and I wear on holiday, but some women wear to work), they can detect a body Sarah O'Hare wouldn't sit next to on the beach.

I once had the desk opposite a woman so drab she was fascinating. I was obsessed with her. Her job was to type out all the readers' letters to the editor. Her daily office look was a lot less interesting: a beige polyester A-line skirt to just below the knee (known as the Stumpy Line), a cream polyester blouse and a fawn V-neck nubbly lambs-wool jumper. This ensemble was set off with American Tan tights and cheap beige low-heel court shoes. And remember, this was a long time before Prada.

But although she was the sartorial equivalent of white noise, Ann always had a jaunty air about her (and if I'd been wearing those tights I'd have been suicidal by morning tea). The other notable thing about her (and believe me, I was noting) was that every lunchtime she disappeared for one hour and came back smiling to herself.

Eventually I found out why – Mrs Beige was the long-term mistress of the most highly paid man on the newspaper. Every day they had each other for lunch at an apartment kept entirely for that purpose. Large quantities of slinky underwear were involved, apparently, and regular gifts of the small sparkling variety.

It explained the post-prandial grin – a femme fatale in 15-deniers was harder to figure out. But figure was the word. The next time I looked at Ann I put aside my pride and prejudice about man-made fibres and realised she had more dangerous curves than a Formula One circuit and legs longer than the Channel tunnel. Attributes that had been entirely visible to Mr Moneybags at first sight.

And we're supposed to believe it's personality that counts.

New shoes blues

Shooooooooes, I need new shoooooes. When I moved to Australia five years ago I had a vast collection. Now I realise that my assortment of footwear, built over twenty years and embracing everything from handmade man-style brogues to stiletto mules with marabou pompoms and leopardskin cowboy boots, is getting smaller.

The problem is that I am wearing shoes out and I can't replace them. I am using up my cobbler's capital. I hate to criticise my adopted homeland, but I am afraid it is a tough fact. It is hard to find good shoes in Australia.

There, I've said it and I've probably let myself in for a lashing of anti-Pom racism, but it's not an opinion inspired by some kind of 'Blighty's better' sentiment — I have can-vassed my Australian-born friends and they feel the same way. The response was unanimous: Australia is the best country in the world (that's why I live here), but the shoes are shithouse.

I don't understand it. We do everything else so well. I love my weekend casuals from Witchery, my urban chic gear from Scanlan & Theodore and my best frocks from Collette Dinnigan. But where am I supposed to get the shoes to go with them?

I love and adore my all-Australian R.M. Williams boots (which inspired wonder at the shoemenders when I had them re-heeled in England last year), so I know that Australians are perfectly capable of making top toecovers, but RMs don't really go so well with lace shifts or sundresses.

I've still got some evening shoes in relatively good shape from my past life, but I am literally running out of shoes to wear to work and I've looked everywhere from the big stores, to the chain stores, the discount dives and the designer dens. Nothing.

In Paris, Milan and even London, you can't leave home without tripping over shoes so enticing you'd swear they could change your life. And not all in name-dropper boutiques, just in 'ordinary' shoe shops. We don't seem to have ordinary shoe shops here.

There is one chain that does affordable shoes which look great, but when you try them on they appear to have been designed by someone who has never seen the human foot. And to be honest, I don't want to walk around in shameless copies of the latest hot shoe from Gucci or Prada, I would like a style with its own integrity. An interpretation of the new trend, not a blatant rip-off.

In both Melbourne and Sydney there are serious shoe booteeks which import the elite of the overseas labels, but I couldn't afford those for everyday wear when I lived in Europe and they cost about one hundred per cent more here.

Price aside – and I've become so desperate I've even considered sandals for $500 – the specific styles they bring in are all a bit too tricksy for my tastes anyway. It's like they have to justify the outrageous price with a big flag waving over the toe saying, 'These are Dee-Zyner shoes.'

I don't want designer shoes. I just want something simple and well-made. Shoes that won't strangulate my toes, won't curl up at the end after two months and don't have linings that adhere to the soles of the feet like sticky-back plastic.

When, in desperation, I told the assistant at one of the high-price salons (who was shifting from foot to throbbing foot on her designer heels), 'I'm just looking for something really plain and comfortable with a medium heel, but well-made and not frumpy . . .' she replied, 'Yes, so is everyone else who comes in here . . . So am I actually . . .'

So why on earth doesn't somebody sell them?

Cracking the dress code

Proust schmoost, yeah yeah, done that. Door knob, madeleine, Odette. Bit of a pervey weirdo. Nice gloves. Next?

War and Peace. Soap-opera simple, darl. Peace. War. Gorgeous snooty Prince bloke dies. Ghastly Pierre lives. Peculiar Freemasons stuff. Snow. Pages of boring war stuff.

The Classics? The Gauls attacked the ditches. The girls sang on the beaches. And these things having been achieved, everyone else pashed their mother, murdered their father and got turned into an olive tree. This is too easy.

Kabbala? Year Seven. I want a challenge. Okay, I'll look at these Christmas party invitations.

'Jacket. Tie optional.'

Well, that's helpful. Are trousers optional too? And what kind of jacket did you have in mind precisely? A Schott

Perfecto leather biker's jacket? A pink hunting coat? A taxi driver's seven-year-old car coat? And pray, what is *she* supposed to wear while he's getting down to 'Jail Break', his suit jacket around his waist, his old school tie around his head? A straitjacket? A jacket potato? More information necessary. And by the way, I'm busy that Thursday.

'Lounge suit.'

Does this mean it is made from upholstery fabric, Von Trapp-style, or are we going to be clicking our fingers to 'Fly Me to the Moon' and 'The Girl from Ipanema' while sipping on a Sea Breeze, daddy-o? Maybe you'll be lying on the lounge in the lounge in your lounge suit, sweetheart, but I'll be at home lying on my sofa in the drawing room in a tracksuit. Goodbye.

'Cocktails. Black tie.'

Well, fine. As long as you're *serving* them. Next question.

'Black tie. 6 pm.'

Uh? Perhaps you could factor in the phone box we're supposed to change in, along with the preposterous dress code. And do tell, what exactly is going to happen at 8 pm, the hour when invitations traditionally start to involve dinner? Are we all going to turn into pumpkins? Miss Alderson regrets. (The only black tie engagement anyone should accept before 7.30 pm is for the Oscars and I have it on good authority that you'll have much more fun watching them at home, dress code: old cardie, than anywhere near the Dorothy Chandler Pavilion.)

'Medieval Mayhem.'

Hello? I'll have two Quattro Formaggios, large, a green salad and an extra-large bottle of Diet Coke. Thank you. What do you mean it will take forty minutes?

'Up.'

Mmmmmm . . . that's more like it. I think I get this. High heels, low front, small dress, big attitude. The only way is . . .

'White tie.'

Mwa, mwa, mwa. At last you speaky my language. He wore: a stiff white bib, a white tie, cutaway tails, decorations, a smug expression. She wore: low on the top, long on the bottom, expensive in between, big hairdo, big jewels, big smile, long white gloves. The consequences were: They could have danced all night.

You can sit on your lounge in your lounge in your lounge suit . . .

. . . . I'll be lounging on my sofa in my drawing room

Goodbye Elton's wig

'What's that on your head?'

This is the opening line from 'Wigs On Fire' by the B52s, one of the best pop songs ever written. The second line is 'A wig', followed closely by a gleeful chorus of 'wig wig wig wig . . .'

It came to mind because I was watching the music channel on pay-the-rich-bloke TV and Sir Elton was on. And all I could think was, What's That On Your Head?

I mean, why would you? If you had all the money in the world and were going to buy a wig, why would you buy a ginger one? It was clearly real hair and a beautiful piece of work, but nothing he was saying, not even the really bitchy stuff about Madonna and the funny stuff about performing nude, could take my mind off the rug on top of his nut.

Because it *was* a-top. It was a hair hat, with those telltale features of an edge-hiding fringe and an unnaturally high crown. Even a wig this expensive was still obviously a flying head carpet and I started to obsess on what he would look like if I had a magic fishing rod and could cast my line into the TV set and hoik the wretched thing off.

Well, I regret to say that Elton without his pelt on would look very much like a fish-and-chip shop owner from Northern England, although that is more to do with the jade tracksuit and large crucifix earring than the visualised Teflon head. The difference is, those things are changeable, whereas it seems that, despite his many and varied efforts, the chrome dome really is not.

I can understand how he feels. I was actually half-bald for a while myself and it wasn't very nice. I had to have radiation beamed at my head for medical reasons and my hair fell out completely, from my neck to just above my ear. Egg.

It was very peculiar and rather chilly and I was greatly relieved when it grew back in wispy little ringlets, although I did have some fun in the meantime frightening children and wearing a lot of hats, in case a gust of wind blew my curtain of hair up to reveal the Empty Quarter beneath.

That experience gave me a great deal of respect for fellow travellers who lose their barnet to radio- and chemotherapy, and if they choose to wear a wig to get them through it, I raise my hairpiece to them.

But while I understand that, like life-threatening tumours, male pattern baldness is very hard to deal with, I really don't believe rugs, weaves, implants, toupees or comb-overs are the answer.

Why can't Sir Elton of John just shave his head and have henna tattoos stencilled onto it? That's what Madonna would do if she started losing it in the thatch department. He could stick purple glittery stars on it to match his suits. He could get his team of florists to create special laurel wreaths for him. It worked for Caligula, it could work for him.

Why can't he see that shaved heads are really sexy? I reckon that singer from Hot Chocolate wrote 'You Sexy Thing' after looking in the mirror when he shaved off the last of his hair. He would never have made it *with* hair.

Or if Elton really can't bear the thought of a stripped scalp, why can't he just wear a funky spunky hat like his old friend Milly Molly Meldrum, country singer Dwight Yoakam and many others of the famous and follicularly challenged fraternity?

The girls in the B52s wore wigs at all times of course. Teased, pigtailed, high on the crown, bouffant all the way in the most unlikely colours, but that was different. They were irono-wigs like drag queens wear and that's the cruel truth, Dorothy. You just can't afford to be seen in an Irish jig you wouldn't take off for a dollar dare.

$\mathcal{L}$ a s t   i n   b e s t   d r e s s e d

There are well-dressed people, there are stylishly dressed people and then there are Best Dressed people. This elite crew, the ones who appear on Best Dressed Lists (BDL), live in a parallel universe. They are not like the rest of us.

To maintain the standards of grooming and attire it takes to get on a BDL, whether it be the 'official' one from New York, or *Harper's Bazaar & Mode*'s annual Aussie version, requires a level of commitment and self-discipline equal to that of an Iron Man, or a shaolin monk.

In other words, you have to be a little nuts.

In the heady Halston days of Studio 54, Best Dressed babe Bianca Jagger used to take a whole day to get ready to go out. She would take Polaroids of herself from different angles to see how she looked. And this wasn't for a special occasion. We're not talking Inaugural Ball, this was every night with the same bunch of drugged-out neurotics she always went out with.

But while Bianca was in those days, like many BDs, married to a walking charge card, being Best Dressed is only partly about money. It's true you'll never make the list in polyester tailoring, but it's as much a matter of priorities as spending power.

It is the enormous proportion of their income they are prepared to spend on their wardrobes that marks out a BD. They'll go into debt to stay well-heeled if they have to and do without little luxuries like owning a car, an apartment, or having children, in order to have their Kelly bags, their Pacific pearl earrings and each season's new Prada shoe.

But another thing that makes BDs different from the rest of us is that they are actually quite happy to have very few clothes – as long as they're the right ones – and they're not sentimental about them. They'll wear a Chanel suit or an Armani evening ensemble constantly for one season and then, chop, get rid of it. Which was why, twice a year, the thrift shops of New York's Upper East Side used suddenly to be full of size six designer clothes. Jackie Onassis was having her new season tax deductible throw-out.

And unlike the rest of us – who treat shopping like an Easter egg hunt, setting off blindly optimistic that we will stumble over something we like, that fits us in our price range – BDs plan their seasonal spends with military precision. They have personal relationships with the managers of the best shops, who ring them when the new stock comes in and put choice pieces aside.

'Mrs Kellogg,' they say. 'We've just received this aqua palazzo pants-suit which we think would be perfect for St Barts. We only have one size four and we're holding it for you.' Then the BDs bowl over and carefully select exactly what they 'need' for business day, casual day, after six, resort and formal evening wear.

And it doesn't end there. Once chosen, it all has to be altered to fit exactly by the special seamstress the BD has cultivated over several years. Not just taking up the sleeves or shortening legs, mind you; the BD will have an entire jacket rebuilt in order to get the perfect line across the shoulder, the precise flatness of a lapel. She'll spend another couple of hundred dollars on a jacket that already cost her $2000.

Then they look after it all like Lord Montagu of Beaulieu looks after his cars. The Turin shroud doesn't get better attention than a BD's wardrobe. One Best Dressed Sydney woman, who is also a mother in full-time work, drives forty-five minutes on Saturdays to and from the only drycleaner in the metropolis she deems capable of properly looking after her clothes. New York BD Nan Kempner sends her gear to *Paris* for pressing.

On a day-to-day basis, it's pure Duntroon. They plan and press what they're going to wear the night before and check it for the stains, loose buttons and dropped hems we all notice on the way to work. They buy imported panty-hose in bulk and keep them in special little embroidered bags. They wash their French lingerie by hand, polish their leather handbags each week and have shoes re-heeled before they quite need it. Legendary New York magazine editor Diana Vreeland (*Harper's Bazaar*, *Vogue*) used to have the *soles* of her shoes polished, because she said it was so 'ordinary' not to.

There is nothing ordinary about being a BD. It's a full-time occupation. They have to fit breathing and feeding themselves around checking hems, steaming jackets and filing spare buttons. Mind you, they're on a permanent starvation diet anyway, to maintain the Duchess of Windsor figure that is an essential part of being a human coat-hanger. (That or plastic surgery.)

All of which makes shaving your head and hanging upside down seem like a perfectly sensible thing to do. As long as you have the new season's saffron robes to do it in, of course.

The joy of specs

Men probably don't make passes at girls who wear glasses, Dorothy was right. But they often promote them or marry them. It works like the brunette thing. They get taken more seriously.

Mind you, it was different in Dot's day. Girls who wore glasses then wore glasses. If they didn't wear them, they would have fallen down holes or ended up sitting next to Mr Magoo on the express train, next stop Fort Apache, the Bronx.

The point being, they didn't have bright blue contact lenses as an alternative back in the 1930s. These days, when a gal wears goggles, it's a style decision. They represent an unmissable opportunity to pay and display yet another designer accessory. No wonder people who don't really need specs ponce around in Armani frames.

People like movie stars, for instance. When it comes to image, nothing they do is just for practicality. People who think that having ribs removed and silicone implants put in their calves are valid tax deductions are not going to baulk at putting a little sliver of plastic in their eyes for instant better eyesight without glasses.

So I reckon when you see a big star in specs, it's all contrived and they have sussed out that glasses can not only enhance your perceived intelligence, they can make you look terribly attractive as well. They can turn a guy from bozo babe magnet into thinking woman's crumpet in one trip to the optometrist.

I don't think Liam Neeson is a twit – he probably really needs his little round horn-rims – but either way, they make him even more dreamy than he is normally. I interviewed him once and blushed like a radish every time he said my name. I still force friends to listen to the tape at dinner parties. He was wearing the glasses. Anyway, whether he needs them or not, those specs make Mr Neeson look like the chemistry teacher who has no idea how gorgeous he is.

But when it comes to others, I'm not so sure. I'm not at all convinced, for example, that Kevin Costner has a rare form of astigmatism that makes spectacles the only thing between him and the wheels of a bus, but I reckon he is smart enough to know how much they suit him. They really set off a dinner jacket and those attractive smiley lines he got around his eyes when he spent all that time out in full sunlight disco-dancing with wolves.

It starts getting really suspect with people like Sylvester Stallone, who would probably say he needs them when he's painting (ha!). We might let Speccy Schwarzenegger off the hook because he *is* married to a Kennedy, so you might trip over the odd book (or copy of *George* magazine) in that house, but I'm certain Bruce 'Four Eyes' Willis hasn't strained his peepers reading much recently, unless it was balance sheets for Planet Hollywood, or Demi's Amex bill.

Come to think of it, I think I've even seen Ms Moore in black-framed geek glasses, trying to make like Jodie Foster (after a lobotomy). Jodie gives good specs. Mind you, she has a big desk, too, and her own production company, so she's allowed to wear them. She actually is intelligent.

But she'd probably find it harder to make people believe it if she wore contacts, being pretty and blonde and that.

Oh solo me, oh

I never could see the point of butterknives, and I'm quite happy not to wear gloves to work, but there is one social convention I would really like to reinstate.

My mother used to call them Spare Men. I really can't think of anything handier. She always had a list of them in her head, and if she didn't have one for a dinner party she would phone around madly until she bagged one. She had Spare Women, too. The idea was — and how quaint it seems — that it was the hostess's responsibility to make sure everyone at a lunch or dinner party had a potential partner to flirt with. Or at least talk to.

No single woman ever sat at my mother's table wondering if there was a single man left anywhere in the world, because there would be at least one sitting next to her. It didn't matter if he looked like a warthog and she loathed him on sight. It just mattered that he was there.

Just at the moment I'm single, okay? Like Noël Coward,

I travel alone. And when I arrive at your house for dinner in a carefully planned outfit and a no-make-up make-up look that took thirty minutes to do, wearing my best scent and carrying an expensive bottle of wine, I would really love it if you had provided a single male for me to sit next to. Preferably one I haven't met.

I'm not saying I want you to lay on some inter-course intercourse, but it would be really nice, just occasionally, to feel I had the chance of meeting a man at a civilised social engagement. As opposed to a mosh pit.

Let me give you an example. One Christmas I was invited to a lovely lunch at Palm Beach. There were three heterosexual couples, three gay couples, about six single gay men. And me. A partridge in a pear tree would have been welcome.

I think it's rude and I think it's lazy, but it happens all the time.

As a reaction, there is a trend among Sydney's solos for singles-only dinners.

They are hideous. Everyone arrives with such tense expectations that the whole thing dissolves almost immediately into vile debauchery brought on by fear-drinking. There is usually a lot of nude disco-dancing and no true social contact.

These Mr Goodbar bacchanals wouldn't be necessary if couples reached out of their comfy smugness for a moment and provided opportunities for spinsters and bachelors to meet with propriety.

In Jane Austen's time, couples seemed to enjoy it. It gave them something to do apart from arguing. Her novels are entirely about the importance of Spare Men. Every social engagement in those days was designed around getting single people together.

Please can we bring that convention back? I can live without calico bonnets, but I sure would love to meet the Duke of Right at dinner.

Why don't you go and get dressed?

It is very easy to underestimate the value of the dress as a garment. I reckon that we women have been so caught up in the excitement of wearing trousers and the this-goes-with-that possibilities of separates that we have forgotten all about dresses. Which is a waste.

But ever since the first suffragette rode her penny-farthing in shocking pantaloons, dresses have seemed too girly, too pappy, too easy. There was almost something shameful to the sisterhood about wearing dresses.

They came to represent a time when we weren't allowed to wear anything else and we wanted to break out and wear our zouave pants and boilersuits and bell-bottoms and knickerbockers and culottes, to prove that we could. Not to forget gauchos, harem pants and that strange garment Olivia Newton-John wore to sing

'Xanadu', half-skirt, half-trouser, fully terrifying. Just watch one re-run of *Rhoda* and you'll see what a bad idea all of those things were.

Even now, when we've calmed down a bit and most of us can wear trousers to work, even air hostesses and nurses (listen, this is all pretty recent, I remember when lady policepersons had to wear skirts), we're still not quite sure about the semiotics of dresses. I think we're still slightly concerned that they might give out Stepford Wife signals, because, let's face it, none of those gingham-clad Martha Stewart clones wore bootleg pants.

So we'll wear dresses for special occasions like high school formals and weddings (as long as we are the bride) and skimpy little numbers to parties, but that's dressing up, not getting dressed. When was the last time you wore a dress to work? And I don't mean that skirt and top your ten-year-old son once described as 'a nice dress', I mean one garment, worn on its own, or with perhaps the small addition of a cardigan in case of draughts.

If you want to be reminded what a good idea dresses can be, get *Breakfast at Tiffany's* out on video again. Do you remember the scene where Holly Golightly is getting ready to go to prison-visiting? She puts on a black sleeveless shift dress, puts on her high heels, puts on her hat and walks out the door. Dressed.

That's what I reckon we should all do. Make getting dressed mean just that again. Okay, so in Holly's case it was a Givenchy dress (when that was still a good thing for a dress to be) and about as fine a pair of high heels as you could ever hope to meet, and she was actually Audrey Hepburn, not just you or me off to work, but the principle is the same.

Getting dressed with a dress is a much simpler prospect than mixing and matching all manner of unrelated garments, which involves more decisions of the colour co-ordination and tucking in or hanging out variety than I am capable of making on a Monday morning.

Dresses bring it down to three decisions. Which dress? Which shoes? Which handbag? And maybe a fourth – which cardigan?

This all came back to me just the other week when I was trying to figure out what you wore to a very chichi birthday party that started at 4 pm on a Sunday afternoon. Hopping around the house at 4.37 pm with a skirt on one leg, trousers on the other and four potential tops thrown on the floor it came to me in a flash. I'll stop trying to create a look and just get dressed. On went the simple bias-cut frock and a pair of strappy sandals, a quick moment with an eyelash curler and there I was, dressed.

I think getting dressed the dress way again could be quite liberating. All men have to think about when they get dressed for work is which suit, which shirt, which tie. Why shouldn't we make it that easy for ourselves? So go on, girls, go and get dressed.

Lost style icons

I hate to introduce a sad note, but there are some people I miss and I want to talk about them.

I miss the Princess. No matter what you think of the whole notion of inherited privilege, don't you miss the splash of her glamour across the news? It was always such a pleasant burst of light relief from the pain, lies and misery of the general news to see the beautiful Princess in her latest gorgeous outfit, just dancing with someone, sporting a new haircut or smiling at an old lady. All she had to do to cheer me up was get a new handbag.

It wasn't until it was taken away that I realised what a tonic she had been all those years. She even knew how to do smart casual in a war zone – remember the Ralph Lauren chambray shirt and jeans in Angola and Bosnia? Which is not to trivialise the impact she made on the landmines issue with those visits, but she just happened to look good while she was doing it. And that was exactly what made those heartbreaking images of limbless children flash around the world so fast. Her glamour helped inspire interest in the cause.

The Princess was a great comfort to all us ageing babes, too. The closer she got to forty, the better she looked. On one of her last public appearances, in that tomato-red shift dress, she looked her best ever, glowing in her maturity. I miss that. When fashion magazines are full of malnourished fourteen-year-old girls, sometimes you need reminding just how beautiful grown women with real baby mama tummies are.

Of course, she didn't always look great. Remember that ghastly, twee sailor collar she wore the first time she came to Australia? But in the last few years of her life, she really developed her own style. Funny to think that, in years to come, fashion magazines will do the 'Princess Di look' in retro photo spreads just as they do with Jackie Onassis.

I miss Jackie O, too. She was wearing Oleg Cassini when I was wearing stretch towelling and it gave me something to aspire to. I don't remember where I was when President Kennedy died, but I can recall precisely where I was when I first shrugged a cashmere cardigan around my shoulders, looped on a big rope of (fake, in my case) pearls and pushed a huge pair of dark glasses on my face. I was late for work. She was one of several reasons I once dyed my hair black. And is still a great excuse to buy shoes in more than one colour.

And I miss Michael Hutchence, too. He had such natural, throwaway, rock-god style. He didn't try to look cool; it just happened. The last time I saw him, at Collette Dinnigan's fashion show in Paris, he was wearing a tight Gucci pinstripe suit with a big tear in one knee. He wore that $4000 suit with the insouciance most men would wear jeans and he made it look as sexy as leather trousers. What a beautiful man he was.

So, with these great gaps in our pantheon of style icons, who do we rush to look at new pictures of now? I couldn't give a flying fig leaf what Sophie Rhys-Jones wore to the Really Useful Company party; Hillary Clinton could have her head shaved and not attract my interest (although I wouldn't mind talking to her about politics); and I don't even know what the lead singer of Savage Garden looks like.

We might have to wait for Prince William to start choosing his own clothes and get married before the real thing comes along again.

The fashion victim diet

I'm wearing a big badge on my shirt today, it says: 'Expand your wardrobe without spending a cent – stop and ask me how.'

It's true, punters, there is an incredibly simple way to double the size of your wardrobe in just four weeks without spending any money. Yes, without entering a single designer boutique, you will have twice the choice of outfits each morning. How?

You just have to lose five kilos.

Instantly you will discover a whole world of clothes which haven't fit you (fat you?) for three years, since the time you got that nasty food poisoning in Katmandu. As well as long-lamented trousers two sizes too small, keyhole bathing suits and tight Lycra dresses, a whole new repertoire of clothing combinations will become available to you. Nifty manoeuvres like tucked-in shirts and belted out-fits, which were off limits while you had to keep up constant stomach, thigh and butt censorship, will once more be part of your world. Getting dressed will become fun again.

All you have to do is lose those pesky little five kilos — which are of course additional to your 'real' weight anyway (which is whatever you weighed at your high school formal). Make this small effort, my friends, and once again you will be able to wear tops which stop dead at the waist, without going on to apologise for your hips.

Now I know it's not easy to lose weight. You keep trying to leave it places, but somehow it always finds its way home. And because I know how hard it is, and because I care deeply about your wardrobes, I have written a diet book which will make losing weight so simple and easy. *The Fashion Victim Diet* is only one page long. Because all diet books boil down to one page. Page 139.

The first 138 pages explain the amazing new discovery that makes this the best diet ever invented, so easy to follow and guaranteed to make superfluous adipose melt like a Paddle-pop in the sun. It might be about the miraculous enzymes in gherkins which cause love handles to wither on impact, a doctoral thesis on liver function with diagrams, or a detailed explanation of why you should eat like a Cameroonian pigmy, because they are never overweight and never suffer from scrotal cancer. They might tell how you can chant yourself thin, or why goose fat makes you gorgeous while chicken fat makes you gross.

Whatever those first chapters say, you will believe it with the zeal felt only by someone who now knows there is a way they'll be back in a bikini by New Year's Day. Then you reach page 139 where it says, You cannot eat peanut butter or drink pinot noir and lose weight on this miracle diet, pigface. Because all diets, whatever their revolutionary secret, boil down to the same thing – you can't get slim and eat and drink the good stuff.

So you can accept that, suffer and regain the full promise of your wardrobe, or you have two other alternatives. You can go and lick pavements in Nepal in the hope of another dose of dalai belly. Or you can go shopping.

See you in Georges.

A great vintage

I miss the old blokes. It was Anzac Day that triggered this off. On the corner of Hunter Street I saw this wonderful old guy. He was wearing the most beautiful grey suit, a regimental tie, a green-and-white polka dot silk handkerchief, polished shoes and a grey felt hat. And, of course, medals. He was carrying a rolled umbrella and standing up straight. No hands had ever been caught lounging in the pockets of that suit. He was so smart. I wanted to shake his hand.

Maybe it was the years in the army that did it, but I really miss the standards of grooming and deportment of my father's generation. They were never scruffy. Even in sailing gear – which in Doug's case (Royal Electrical Mechanical Engineers) was Levi's, a Guernsey sweater, canvas deck shoes and a Greek fisherman's cap – they were relaxed, but there was always a standard. His friend Max Savage (Merchant Navy) had wonderful old brick-red sailing trousers and a sailing smock. These were ancient garments, but they weren't tacky. They were one's sailing clothes. No socks of course, but clean fingernails.

They had a sense of style without being gimmicky, that generation. It was like they decided at a certain point what they were going to wear, had the suits made by their tailor, stocked up on shirts and sweaters as necessary and that was it. Clothes were done. Although there was always room for a bit of fun with silk handkerchiefs and racy ties.

Doug's great friend Don Munro (Royal Engineers, Burma) used to buy him saucy ties as a joke. I remember one involving something called the White Anchor sailing club which they thought was hilarious (something about W. Anchor which I didn't understand in 1970). Don had a great look. A navy suit with a special longer-line jacket, handmade shirts, various ties and dark brown suede chukka boots. I think he used to wear red cashmere socks as well, but it was the boots that did it for me. So cool.

Walter Dean (Royal Engineers) was another one. Always immaculate. Beautiful suits, hair always cut and groomed. He would no more have let his hair grow to his collar than fail to stand up when a lady entered the room. You know that gorgeous thing when they bob up from the chair every time you get up? I don't care how old-fashioned it is, it makes me feel good.

They haven't all gone of course. Spencer Copeland (Cavalry, Royal Engineers) is always perfectly turned out.

When I visited his house in Cornwall last year he was wearing a lovely grey suit to show people around his china collection, and when they had gone he disappeared for a moment and then came back wearing a burgundy cashmere cardigan instead of the jacket, so he could be more comfortable for tea. I swooned. He's seventy-something. He still skis.

I think it must have been partly a result of the rather extreme level of discipline at school in their day, combined with the compulsory army experience, that gave the WWII generation the standards of attire they stuck to for life, but that's not to say these guys were all stitched-up old fascists. They were all charming and twinkly (Spencer still is) and, certainly in the case of Don and Doug, could tend towards the wild if they felt like it.

Doug was a petrol-head at Brooklands in the 1930s. Don used to sail to America for fun. They both had sports cars way past the age they said they would and they loved a boys' trip to Cardiff Arms Park or Murrayfield for the rugby (they once drank an Edinburgh hotel dry of Dom Perignon, but that's another story). So they certainly weren't stuffy. But they never hung up a tie still knotted and they never, ever wore unpolished shoes.

Travelling lite

As you know, I'm the kind of twit who packs five cardigans and six pairs of shoes for a weekend in the country, but there have been occasions when I have travelled light, honestly there have. On more than one trip I have heard the blissful words, 'Is that all you've got?' in relation to my luggage, as opposed to the more usual, 'What have you got in here? Dead bodies?'

Obviously if you're going island-hopping around Greece, or backpacking in Vietnam, it makes sense to leave four of the cardigans at home, but there's more to travelling light than just taking less than you want to. It's a state of mind and it's one which you can apply just as easily to a visit to New York, London or Paris as two weeks on the beach in Bali. Some people are born with it, but you can learn it.

The secret is this: only take one of any garment type. One shirt, one short, one pant, one cardie, one pair of shoes, that's it. For the city trips you'll substitute a cashmere shawl for your sarong and a tailored jacket for your favourite old linen shirt, but the theory is the same.

It may sound impossible, if not insanitary (One T-shirt? Is she kidding?), but don't you find that you end up wearing the same thing every day on holiday anyway? To travel light, that's all you take. The things you wear every day. You don't take the ones you normally leave in the suitcase, get it?

And if you can force yourself to do it, minimalist packing has bonuses way beyond the practical considerations of hopping on and off boats and planes and trains and buses with three suitbags, a hatbox and a Louis Vuitton shoe trunk. It gives you an incredible lightness of being along with the incredible lightness of luggage, because it frees you from the worry of wondering what you should wear.

You can't worry about it because you don't have any choice. For anyone who regularly re-carpets their bedroom floor with clothes in the search for something to leave the house in, that is very liberating. It also makes you very creative with what you do have.

On a trip around Turkey with my boyfriend and one very small bag, we drove from banana plantations and camels on the southern coast to the central city of Konya in one day. It was dusk when we got to Konya. It was also snowing. I soon figured out why the city's famous Whirling Dervishes wear trousers underneath their skirts. To keep warm.

After five minutes as a styling Dervish in my hotel room I emerged ready to explore Konya by night, wearing: Birkenstock sandals, socks, leggings, a swim-suit, a T-shirt, a sundress, a shirt, a cotton cardigan, a bandana tied round my head like Willie Nelson and a sarong wittily draped as a shawl. Gee, was I cosy. The only garment left lying on the bed was my shorts.

And the funny thing was that, while I wouldn't want to wear that particular outfit strolling along Boulevard St Germain, it didn't look as bag-lady nuts as it could have, because everything was navy, with red and white accents in the bandana and sarong. I also kept telling myself (and anyone else who would listen) that Dries Van Noten had recently had a big moment with pants under dresses, so it was quite a valid look that season anyway.

Which is more than can be said for the socks-tucked-into-baseball-cap ear-warmer ensemble dreamed up by the BF the same evening. He got some very funny glances, but as he said, with the assurance of one of life's natural light packers, at least he had warm ears.

I wouldn't want to wear that particular outfit strolling along Boulevard Saint Germain

The power of one packing system

Okay, having established that it is possible even for a cardigan-fixated, shoe-obsessed twit like me occasionally to travel light, let's break this down a bit. I'm going to share with you my packing master list for casual, hot weather holidays.

This is designed according to my previously explained Power of One Packing System, which is based on the understanding that you can only take *one* example of any garment type (this includes cardigans) and that your whole travelling wardrobe should be *one* colour, with bright accents.

I worked this out by keeping notes of what I actually wore on trips and anything I bitterly regretted leaving at home on the bed, and then referring to these notes when packing for the next holiday. For a while this meant I was always perfectly equipped for the previous expedition, but after a few years of refinement (and borrowing clothes from other people on holiday) I came up with the master list. It works for me.

The Master List

One pair of shoes – either sandals or trainers
One pair of shorts
One T-shirt
One sarong
One pair of light pants *or* leggings
One shirt
One jumper *or* one cardigan
One hat
One swimsuit
One sundress (optional for men, who can substitute a
   second shirt or T-shirt)
One pair of socks
One set of undies
One bandana
One feature necklace
One shoulder bag

Just for fun, put that little pile on your bed and thrill at how tiny it is. Then consider that when you get on the plane you will be wearing the pants, T-shirt and shirt, with the trainers or sandals on your feet, the jumper around your shoulders, the necklace around your neck, the undies on your bottom, the hat on your head and the bandana around that. So your little bag will contain only the shorts, the sundress, the socks and the sarong. Wow. And a bumper-sized tube of Travelwash.

You will be amazed how many different outfits you can get out of this micro-wardrobe. Especially if you think outside the square when you choose the items. The sundress doesn't have to be a flowery thigh flipper, it can just as easily be a bias-cut ankle-length column that is comfortable to wear drifting around ruins in the day and perfect for lounging around in with an ouzo at night. With the shirt knotted over it, it will be very chic; with the cardigan, quite cosy.

The bandana and the sarong/shawl are two of your key items — don't think of them as mere accessories, they are survival kits. They can be used as towels, picnic rugs, beach mats, tablecloths, turbans, bandages, tents, fan belts and so on. I couldn't conceive of going away without my red bandanna; it is totemic. It brightens up my favourite navy linen shirt and trouser ensemble and looks just as good tied round my straw stetson as it does around my neck. When I'm feeling really up myself I knot it around the handle of my shoulder bag. *Ça c'est bon, monsieur.* Fwa fwa fwa.

When it comes to the travelling shoe, if you are going to be doing major bushwalking you would tend towards the trainer, and my friend Seb says he has also found them very effective as a security wallet. He travelled all round

South-East Asia with his parents' American Express card sewn into the inner sole of his Nikes, for emergencies. Even in the roughest backpacker accommodation he knew it was safe, because no-one with normal nasal functioning would deliberately approach one of his trainers.

For exactly that reason I'm a great fan of the holiday Birkenstock. No matter that they used to be worn only by vegans (they remind them of lunch) and chiropractors, they are still a backless shoe, which makes them a mule in my book. Perfectly painted red toenails spark them up a treat. Away from home I'll even wear them with socks. See if I care.

About your holiday hat. Packing purists would take only a rollable Panama straw or cotton sunhat, but I go the other route, which is the hat you wear all the time. As I am quite prepared to wear it in public at Mascot airport, this means my trusty straw stetson can come everywhere with me. Nothing beats it for keeping off the sun, and it is also handy for carrying fruit and giving water to a thirsty horse.

If you are going to a location where there could be a sudden drop in the temperature, try packing a pair of 15-denier tights. They take up no room and can provide an amazing layer of warmth under the pants. But please don't wear them with your shorts.

As for your choice of colour theme, I have always found navy ideal. My bandana, as mentioned, is red; my sarong is red, white and blue stripes; and sometimes I go crazee and take a red cardigan. It just works. I do advise against choosing white as your main colour, and I consider two weeks not wearing black a holiday in itself. The only place I deviate from this colour code is my sundress, which is a long sage-green slip by Ghost which looks gorgeous with navy. My Birkenstocks, regrettably, are the same colour as Weet-Bix. I am currently on a global search for a pair of red ones.

Feeling crumby

I am not a monkey. Can we please be clear about that? I am not a monkey, so please don't groom me. Well, maybe if we are curled up on the sofa on a chilly Sunday afternoon watching an old movie and eating shortbread biscuits you can groom me a bit. But not in public, OK?

So if you see me at a cocktail party and I have a blonde hair on the shoulder of my black jacket, can you please leave it there? It's my hair and I want it. I've got plans for it. And if I have a little crumb of sourdough bread on my other shoulder I probably put it there specially and I don't need you to invade my personal space and brush it off. OK?

And that biro mark you have just noticed on my new cream skirt, please don't prod me on the leg and tell me about it. Nobody knows about it more than me. I don't need reminding that I dropped a nasty blue ballpoint pen on my favourite skirt. It is as indelibly inscribed on my heart as it is on the double layer chiffon.

I'm not sure why I object to these pickings and pokings so much, but they make me feel completely invaded. Maybe I'm turning into Howard Hughes, because I am quite fussy about who touches me, but some people seem to think it's open slather. I don't kiss my work mates good morning, for example, and I could get arrested if I touched one of them on their bottom in the office, because it is not considered appropriate behaviour. But apparently it is perfectly acceptable to touch someone's chest in any situation, as long as there is a stray bit of cornflake resting on it.

Well, it's not OK with me and I suspect it's not OK with most of you either.

In fact I think flicking someone else's scurf off the shoulders of their jacket, or pointing out a little soiling in their attire is about the rudest thing you can do. It's got such a know-all air to it and implies with a bright smile and a brush of a hand, 'You really aren't very well groomed, are you?' Well, I'm sick of being patrolled by the self-appointed grooming police and on behalf of all of us natural-born filth packets, I am asking them to stop it.

They don't restrict themselves to remarking on temporary specks either; some of them will happily pass comment on the fundamental state of your garments. Such a woman once pointed out to me that the fabric was worn away on the front of one of my Patrick Cox satin loafers.

I already knew it was worn away, it was from driving, but I couldn't bear to stop wearing them because they were so nice when I bought them. It was none of her business if they were old and crappy and now, because buying shoes is like a marriage. Long after they have become crumpled and scuffed, you still see them the way they were when you first met.

She wouldn't have come up and told me, 'Your partner is looking a bit lined, isn't he?' But she felt it was perfectly fine to insult my shoes.

And what makes these bossy people assume that we aspire to their compulsive obsessive standards of personal care anyway? If they want to spend half their income on drycleaning and several hours a day holding a lint roller, that is their choice. I'd rather read a good book. Preferably one covered in fly splats and coffee rings.

I simply don't aspire to look like the kind of woman who has so much time on her hands she can spend all morning sponging her outfit before venturing forth to the manicure parlour. I'm happy to look like I work for a living. Dammit, I'm proud of it.

So the next time someone picks a bit of fluff from my sleeve I'm going to pick it right up and put it back. Or better still, I will howl and gibber like a crazed baboon. That should stop them.

Beyond the pale

We are all damaged goods. Sun-damaged goods. How can you avoid it in this solar-powered country? Even hands that have lived here only a few years tell the story: wrinkles, crinkles and brown spots. After just three Australian summers, the backs of my hands looked older than my sister's. She's seven years my senior. And big on gardening. The difference is that she lives in England, where they still have an ozone layer, and I live here, where we don't.

Sun damage is so endemic in Australia that it's become part of life. It affects our perception. Here, where it's normal for teenagers to have crow's feet, people who have grown up in darker corners of the world find themselves judged much younger than their passports admit.

I arrived from gloomy old Eeyore Britain with skin that rainy summers had left relatively unscarred. But now the relentless fingers of UV have left their indelible marks across my forehead.

And I'm not talking about skin damage that is the just dessert of days baking at Bondi or sizzling at Sorrento. If I go anywhere near a beach, I'm swathed like Lawrence of Arabia, coated in unguent like the dead girl in *Goldfinger*, wearing a broad-brimmed stetson and sitting under an umbrella (oh, the joys of the open-air life).

The new lines on my face are merely the result of the morning walk, the few minutes at lunchtime getting a sandwich, waiting for a taxi, driving the car, walking up Oxford Street on Saturday. Incidental sun exposure. And this is a brow that never leaves the house without sunblock. Factor 15 at least, even on cloudy days (UV this fierce laughs at cloud cover), despite derision from some of my Aussie friends, who consider the use of daily sun protection on a par with drinking decaffeinated coffee and low-alcohol wine. They don't seem to mind that people occasionally mistake them for frill-necked lizards.

But those of us who do attempt to protect our skin from this unnatural assault should pray to the high, hot heavens that the expensive sunblock we smear on daily is doing a better job at protecting us from skin cancer's deadly creep than it is at protecting us from wrinkles.

Apparently, one of the problems is that it wears off, so even if you have plastered it on in the morning, by lunchtime you're as ready for a grilling as a piece of John Dory at Doyles. You've got to apply and reapply the stuff, the beauty editors now tell us.

But before you even start to grapple with the tricky details of application, you've got to find a sunblock that doesn't make you look as if you're auditioning for Marcel Marceau. Some of them go on as pure chalk, others pure grease. Just ask my flatmate. At twenty-three, he's fair-skinned and smooth-browed, and he wants to stay that way. So, every morning he leaves the house looking as though he's trying out to be the next man in the moon. Shiny.

He's got beautiful skin as a result, except when it's covered in spots caused by hopelessly clogged pores. No wonder they call it sunblock, he says.

If the shoe fits...

I once knew a man who had only one pair of shoes. Tom wasn't poor, that was just the way he did shoes, because he hated loathed detested shopping. So every year on October 1, he would go and buy a new pair of black Doc Martens. He would walk out of the shop in them, leaving the old pair behind, and then he'd wear them every single day, without polishing, without mending, without even replacing broken shoelaces, until annual shoe day came around again.

Even with this fail-safe system – same shoe, same size, same shop – he still dreaded it. About the middle of September he would start grumbling about having to buy new shoes and how hideous it was going to be. He hated shopping that much.

Troubled by his distress (and the terrible state of his shoes from August onwards), I wasted a great deal of breath trying to explain to Tom that if he bought two identical pairs of shoes next October 1 and wore them on alternate days, putting shoetrees in on the rest day, he wouldn't need to buy any new shoes until two-and-a-half, possibly three years later.

All shoes need a day off after they have been worn, I told him. They need to breathe and rest their leather generally have a little lie down. They will last more than twice as long if you give it to them. I even offered to buy him the shoe-trees, but he couldn't handle the concept of having more than one pair of shoes in the house. Imagine that.

A lady I met in Sydney told me about a similar system she developed as a bright young gal in the 1950s, struggling to make her way in life on a salesgirl's meagre wage. Rather like Tom, Isabella would buy the same pair of shoes each year. The difference was that hers were Bally stilettos and she had to save up like mad to have them.

Each spring she would buy a pair in white. She'd wear them to work every day, walking into the city from Edge-cliff because the saving on the bus fare went towards the shoe fund. When autumn rolled around and they began to look a bit scuzzy, she dyed them black and carried on wear-ing them every day until she had saved up enough shoe money from bus fares and missed dinners for the next pair. She polished them every night and when they got wet she stuffed them with newspaper to keep them in shape.

I am happy to say that Isabella is now a woman of means and has a glorious shoe closet devoted to beautiful stilettos in every colour and pattern which she has bought all over the world. Some of them she has hardly ever worn, but, after all those years of scrimping, she still appreciates every pair and is very generous about passing them on to the less footwear-privileged.

Isabella deserved to get on in life, because she knew it was better to save up for one good pair of shoes a year than hoof around in three or four different ones of inferior quality. But if only she could have had two pairs of shoes. They could have lasted her so much longer.

My art collector friend, Amanda, has two pairs of shoes. Just the two. Not because she has to scratch the cash together for them, but because she hates clutter. She doesn't really have furniture either; it's so messy and gets in the way of the art.

So she has two pairs of shoes on a revolving system, although in her case there's no particular calendar to the changing of the guard. Instead, it works like this – when she finds a new pair of shoes she likes enough to buy, one of the other pairs has to go. Outski. Bang.

It works for her, just as Tom's and Isabella's shoe systems worked for them. But I think I'll just stick to my own footwear philosophy. As many as possible, until death do us part.

Secret clothes

I was once invited to a dinner party where you had to bring your secret food fetish. Around that table there were dog biscuits, uncooked cake mix, maraschino cherries, strawberry jam and stilton cheese, dry cereal, baked beans (eaten out of the tin), condensed milk (sucked from the tube) and advocaat.

How much more fun it would have been if the dress code had matched the menu. Imagine if you had to wear in public the magnificently hideous garment you secretly love slipping into, but would be horrified if anyone saw you wearing. The kind of garment my native New Yorker friend Karen calls a *schmatte*. Which is Yiddish for rag.

We all know what Cherie Blair's is. What's yours?

Well, I'm prepared to admit it. I would have been sucking on my condensed milk in my pink Mexican dress. It is basically a bright fuschia embroidered kaftan – but not nearly as nice as that makes it sound.

It is made of cotton which hasn't softened with wash and wear, and age has not wearied the hardness of the colour. It stops mid-calf, has sticky-out short sleeves, an unflattering boatish neckline and a yoke *above* the bust, a cut guaranteed to make Jodie Kidd look bulbous. It's a Hattie Jacques of a dress. Plus it's way too big for me, but it was the only pink one in Merida and I had to have it. I love that dress. I shrug it on at the weekend and immediately feel like someone's mad aunt. It's very freeing. I'd die if anyone saw me in it. I'm wearing it now.

Well, that's me. To find out what the truly chic wear off duty, I rang some of Australia's fashion authorities and asked what they wear when we're not looking.

Deborah Thomas, editor of *Cleo* magazine, previously a Paris catwalk model and former editor of *Elle* and *Mode*: 'A bright turquoise chenille dressing-gown with giant daisies all over it. I saw it in the window of a shop in Melbourne and what clinched it is that Fran Drescher has a similar one in *The Nanny*. Of course, when I have visitors I wear the tasteful blue-and-white striped one . . .'

Belinda Seper, eponymous boutique owner and chief womenswear buyer for Georges, Melbourne, and a fixture on Best Dressed Lists: 'My mother just looks at me aghast. Is this the woman who is supposed to be among Sydney's best dressed? I have old sweatshirt pants from agnès b. from ten years ago which are well past their use-by date, but they are so much a part of my emotional wardrobe, I can't part with them. Then, of course, there are the famous old red cashmere socks with holes in them that you wear when you think nobody loves you.'

Collette Dinnigan, fashion designer of international repute: 'I've got a big old white nightdress with pintucks and embroidery. It's quite short. I wore it down to the beach once.'

Jane Roarty, former fashion director of *marie claire* magazine, now editor of *marie claire maison*: 'A huge red stripey kaftan I bought on the island of Zanzibar. It hides every conceivable sin and I can roll around the house in it. You have to totally live the part. It's exotic, it's totally comfortable and I also feel it's historic. I see myself as Madame Guggenheim.'

Karin Upton Baker, the always immaculate editor of *Harper's Bazaar & Mode*: 'It's too awful. It's so shocking I'm not even sure I can speak. For years I have bought my slippers at White Ivy in Double Bay. Quilted white satin. Well, they wore out and I just haven't had time, so I have resorted to a pair of clear plastic thongs that I bought to wear in the showers at a health spa. There is kind of a sparkle through them and they did have large daisies on them, which I had my husband remove with pliers. They are hideous. Every time I put them on I think I must do something about them . . . but I've been wearing them for six months.'

Too easy pieces

The young have it so easy these days. Eee by gum when I were a lass we had to whittle our own clogs. We had to knit party dresses out of sacks. We shared one pair of socks between sixteen of us. And we were lucky. We had socks.

Well, it wasn't really that bad, but we didn't have any of this Portmans and Witchery luxury that young groovers have today. What we had was op shops, jumble sales, army disposal and the occasional miracle find in a cheap chain store, because in those days they only sold trendy clothes in trendy shops and trendy shops were incredibly expensive. So if you wanted to be fashionable you had to be creative. Or rich.

My fashion bible was a book called *Cheap Chic,* which was all about dying nurses' uniforms purple and sewing rickrack onto old cardigans. Even *Vogue* had a special section called 'More Dash Than Cash', devoted to looking fabulous in army shorts and grandpa's spencer. Now, all you need to look fashionable on a budget is full command of the words, 'I'll take it.' In the 70s you had to work for style (and I don't mean a paper round).

Take something as prosaic as a pair of Doc Martens. When I was twenty, they didn't make them in women's sizes and I really wanted some to go with my black jeans (home dyed; you couldn't get black jeans), cast-off cardigan (embroidered with pearls by *moi*) and op-shop old man's jacket (I couldn't afford a new tailored jacket).

Eventually, I did find some miniature Docs in a dusty old school outfitters, but that was after I had been to every shoe shop and disposal store in Dundee. You had to be tenacious to be trendy in 1979. Now you can get Doc Martens for babies. You can get J.P. Tod's for toddlers.

These days, the buyers do all the legwork for us and you don't even need to make it to a proper fashion store to be in style. If you hit Coles on the right day, you can find something really tasty, like a pale pink, stretch towelling dress shaped like an elongated polo shirt, which is the best possible thing to wear over your cossie all summer. It will cost you about $30. You really couldn't find anything better to wear to the beach at Versace or Gucci.

Mind you, if you are really stuck on the latest designer styles, you can just run into Sportsgirl and pick up the most terrific 'interpretations' – sometimes before the real thing has even arrived at the import boutiques – for about one per cent of the designer price.

Twenty years ago, this would have been a fantasy. So Saturdays were a ritual of jumble sales and trawls through my favourite charity shops. It was a challenge. You had to have a real eye for it and when you found something great for fifty cents hidden among a big pile of cack, it was incredibly thrilling.

I can still remember some of my best-ever hauls, like the Salvation Army jumble sale where I scored a never-worn 1950s school mac in navy blue gaberdine and three pairs of ladies' shoes from the 1920s – in my size. At another, I found a bias-cut crêpe dress from the 1930s which could have been tailored for me, and in a charity shop, a Harris tweed sportscoat which had hand-made fishing flies pinned behind the collar.

But although it thrills me that I can now find a perfect agnès b. 'inspired' cardigan at Country Road (rather than trying to make one out of a pair of long johns), this eat-as-much-as-you-like smorgasbord of fashion shopping has taken some of the fun out of the chase. If it's that easy, you just don't want it so much.

Platform shoes

'Oh darling, please wear your highest platform shoes, you know how I love you in them . . .'

No-one has ever said this. It is one of the few fashion pronouncements that men, small children and mothers actually get right – high platform shoes are hideously ugly.

Yet every few years – the 1940s, the 1970s, the early 1990s, the early mid-1990s, the late mid-1990s – they come back into vogue and even relatively normal women feel left out unless they victim around in them for a bit.

Then one day we look in the mirror and realise we are wearing surgical boots. Op shops fill with mini-Stonehenges of monolithic shoes. The madness has passed for a while.

Right now they aren't strictly speaking in fashion (whatever *that* is), or at least they weren't last week, yet the streets are still full of girls clomping around looking like they have bricks attached to their feet. Why?

Well, there are the fashion throwbacks of course. Just as you still see men who have worn brothel creepers continuously since 1959, their faces now as crepey as their soles, there are women who have clung to their platforms as a boho statement ever since David Bowie bit them on the bum in 1972. Ziggy plays guitarrrr. He also wore stupid shoes and some people are determined to preserve the moment. If you really want to dress like a fossil there are always obscure outlets where you can get this stuff.

But what about people young enough to know better? There is the because-they-make-me-look-taller argument, which works brilliantly as long as you stand behind a bar all day. Otherwise it takes just one downward glance to reveal you are just a short person wearing tall shoes. Men have been known to flee at such moments of revelation, with the same sense of shock experienced by Julie Christie when the red duffle coat turned round in *Don't Look Now*. Like Venice in winter, big platforms are really spooky.

Of course very high heels – which are hugely in fashion now, or they were yesterday – are scary too, especially when worn with leather miniskirts, but at least they lengthen your calves and tip your hips into a fatty-bum-bum tilt, which is rumoured to be alluring. Because as you teeter you wiggle. That's it. It's painful, it's stupid, but it *is* sexy. Platforms just make you walk like Herman Munster.

If Marilyn Monroe had been wearing platforms rather than deliberately mismatched stilettoes (apparently she had the heels sawn to different heights specially to give her *that* walk) when she shimmied down to the jetty in *Some Like It Hot*, she would have caused a tidal wave. Rather than nuclear fission.

Platform shoes are also dangerous. Footwear that can bring such a catwalk veteran as Naomi Campbell crashing down to earth should be issued with a Government Health Warning. Something along the lines of: Man, these shoes is *mean*.

And if that still isn't enough to put you off being a career clompasaurus, just consider the rollcall of people famously associated with platform shoes. Elton John, in his novelty spectacles period. KISS. Gary Glitter. Princess Margaret. The Spice Girls.

Baby Spice twisted her ankle falling off her high-rise shoes at Royal Ascot and made the front page of *The Times*. Now don't those ten-centimetre spike heels suddenly look attractive?

Please wear your platforms, darling... you know how much I love them

In a lather

Thank you for asking me, but I'm afraid I won't be able to come out for the next few weeks. I'm rather busy as a little white stranger was delivered this morning. It is five years since I have heard the patter of a tiny spin cycle in my own home and I'm staying in to bond with Ben.

Ben Dix the washing machine, that is. He is my new pride and joy and I won't be happy until every garment, towel, sheet and table cloth I own has passed through his porthole door and come out clean and fresh and smelling of the free fabric conditioner he brought with him.

When my parents first got an automatic washing machine, in about 1970, they pulled up chairs to watch it go round, washing and rinsing and spinning all by itself. They thought it was miraculous (no more mangle!). I thought they were nuts, but now I'm trying to figure out how I can get the sofa into the bathroom so I can watch Ben perform the cold wash in comfort. And I can't wait for that climactic moment when he switches from spinning to drying. Because Ben is a combined unit. He can wash and dry all on his own.

That's why he cost the price of a one bedroom unit in Perth.

Apart from his technical wizardry (he heats up his own water and judges the minimum amount he can use for each load completely unaided, because he cares deeply about the environment), Ben represents a return to adulthood for me, after half a decade living in units that simply could not accommodate any white goods beyond a fridge and a toaster.

For that time my Saturdays have been a trudge of humungous bags in and out of lifts to communal laundries, only to find all the machines were already full. Or having got up at 7.00 am to secure one, of going back an hour later to find my pile of precious clothes suppurating on top of the dryer while someone else's gear purred smugly inside.

In one building where we had a rooftop washing line, I came back to check on my non-fast darks load, to find a woman moving my damp whites out of the sunshine into a dank corner in favour of her own, because hers was 'wetter'. I went back later and threw a pair of her knickers off the roof. After that I stopped hanging my stuff out to dry for fear of reprisals, so it was a choice of festooning it around the flat, like the rags at the site of a recent vision of the Virgin Mary, or nuking it in the communal driers.

They certainly do the job (John Olsen could fire pots in them), but the process involves first taking the pubic lint out of the dryer after someone else's turn, which makes me feel sick. Irrational I know, because it is all freshly washed (otherwise it wouldn't be in the dryer, would it?). But I don't want to touch other people's sock fluff and underscunder plunder at any stage of the wash cycle.

Mind you, at least the apartment buildings here have laundries. In London you have to go to a public laundrette. The horror, the horror. The last time I ever used one I saw a man inspect a pair of trousers he was about to wash, then take off the ones he was wearing and put them in a machine instead. And believe me, he looked nothing like the bronzed love god in the Levi's commercial.

Mad aunt disease

I have on occasion in this book made reference to a type called a 'mad aunt'. I wish to make it clear that this is in no way a derogatory term. In fact, it is one of my dearest ambitions. It is a nirvanic state I have been working up to for some years and hope to realise fully around my sixty-second birthday.

Once I am officially a Mad Aunt, I won't have to worry about smart casual or having the right shoes ever again. I'll be able to wear kaftans, smocks and Dalai Lama robes every day. Bold artisanal jewellery will be my signature and I'll wear espadrilles to drinks parties.

I never had a Mad Aunt of my own, but the nearest would have been a tiny Austrian lady called Lottie who was a friend of my parents. I was very impressed with her because she had once lived in a cave, and although I didn't meet her many times she was a crucial formative influence through the clothes she passed on to me for dress-ups.

Her empire-line bottle-green velvet cocktail dress and ebony cigarette holder were the basis of my Cruella De Vil outfit, using a bottle of Quink ink to dye one side of my hair black.

Even better was a 1950s palm tree print jumpsuit with clambaker legs (just below the knee, with turn-ups), a cinched-in waist and a Miami designer label. I loved to imagine on what kind of occasions Lottie would have worn it, because there certainly wasn't much call for it in rural England. I could see her in a cartwheel hat, cat's-eye sunnies and mules, clip-clopping around pink Art Deco hotels carrying a lavish cocktail. Mad Aunts always have a glamorous past.

They also have a significant place in literature, first catching my attention in a book called *Auntie Robbo*. The character of the aunt, as described by her eight-year-old nephew, is in her seventies, and considers it quite normal to travel around Scotland in a gypsy caravan wearing a Sherlock Holmes coat and deerstalker hat at all times. She is also fearless and very good at catching robbers. I thought she was heaven.

Of course, the great Mad Aunts of the modern era are the Two Fat Ladies of the TV cooking show. So what if the food is vile, I would much rather watch them than those anorexic neurotics on *Friends*. In The One Where They Cook for Boy Scouts and Go Camping, we see Jennifer Paterson throw a piece of used kitchen paper on the ground. She seems a bit surprised herself and then explains, 'I'm throwing it on the ground because it's there.'

Satisfied, she continues making her frittata, a dish with more animal fats than the Royal Easter Show. She doesn't care; she always wears capacious sailing smocks in bright colours and stretch trousers. That's it, that's what she wears. Whether she is cooking for Ghurkhas, attending a cocktail party in Belgravia, or riding round London on her motorbike, that's what Jennifer wears.

Another jewel of a moment in the same episode is a sudden cut to a close-up of her currant-bun face, which is swathed in a tight black hood, while she sips on a restorative cocktail. 'It's my motorcycle helmet bag,' she says happily. 'Got to keep away these blasted midges.'

This total lack of concern for her appearance is quintessentially Mad Aunt – especially when combined with her always beautifully painted nails, dyed black hair and permanent red lipstick. Which show she obviously does care about her appearance, it's just that she has her own rules for it.

I can hardly wait.

Acknowledgments

At last I get to write my Oscar acceptance speech . . .

Of course I want to thank everybody I have ever met and all of Rabbit's friends and relations, but as this book is a collection of journalism I would particularly like to acknowledge all the wonderful people I have met through my profession.

Firstly, Fenella Souter, editor of *Good Weekend*, who made this book possible by asking me to write a column called Style Notes for her magazine, which forms the basis of this book. And Jane Wheatley, deputy editor of the same magazine, who understands, far better than most, the importance of a single word to a writer.

One of the great privileges of my life generally has been the extraordinary mentors I have had. Without them, I wouldn't be writing this. To my great sadness, two of the most crucial ones are no longer here to read it.

Les Daly gave me my big break by offering me work experience on *Options* magazine when I had just left university. No one could write coverlines like Les, one of the few journos to have worked on both *The Sunday*

Times and *The Sun*. What's more, he was utterly respected at both (possibly because he had the most acid wit ever to come south from Scotland). I have even forgiven him for making me write an article called 'Who's Got the Best Bum In Britain?'. Thank you, Les. We all still miss you.

The other late, lamented mentor is John Leese, a truly great editor I worked with at *You* magazine and the *Evening Standard*. I don't think he ever got enough credit in his lifetime, but then, he never went looking for it. John was much more interested in talking to his own journalists than power-lunching the great and the good. He hired other people to do that and took us lot out to Scribes.

John understood brilliantly the dynamics of a team, gave original writers total freedom, paid people what they deserved and so believed in safeguarding editorial integrity that he didn't allow advertising reps to talk to his journos. Like all great editors, he was also very quirky and surrounded himself with eccentrics. The odder the group of people in morning conference, the happier he was. He adored dogs and hated men with beards. He gave me the opportunity to work on Fleet Street when it still was Fleet Street, which was pretty special. What an honour to have known and worked for such a man.

I would also like to thank the following mentors, protégés, friends and colleagues:

Josephine Fairley, for always having total faith in me and being a wonderful friend, editor, contributor and careers advisor. She gave me my first proper job on a magazine and, later, the one I had dreamed of since I was fourteen – features editor of *Honey*.

Alastair Fairley, for taking one look at me and recruiting me for the St Andrews University newspaper. For introducing me to his sister. And for giving the dinner party where I met Les Daly.

Genevieve Cooper, who taught me more about writing than anybody, by making me understand what makes an original voice and how to spot a cliché at twenty yards (Genevieve would put her blue pencil straight through that phrase, for example).

Barbie Boxall, the ultimate sticky bud, who was a great editor herself, but who met me as an equal when I was just a beginner and taught me so much. And thank you, Barbie, for sharing Rose with me.

Ruby Millington (sticky bud two) and Caris Davis, for the most fun I ever had at work, when we were doing Metropolis at the *Evening Standard*. 'Michael plans a few meet 'n' greets with local residents before the Wembley shows' etc. still does it for me.

Fay Maschler, for taking me to The Connaught for lunch (among other places) and remaining a friend long after I left the *Standard*.

My best friends: Karen Moline, E. Jane Dickson and

Josephine Fairley (again), who are all wonderful writers, and Victoria Killay, who isn't published – yet – but who is actually funnier than any of us.

Geoff Laurence, who can write volumes with one stroke of his brush and draw perfect circles without looking.

Jane de Teliga, Wendy Squires and Mia Freedman, my new journo best friends in Australia. And dearest William, who wasn't a journalist when I met him, but certainly is now.

Lisa Wilkinson and Richard Walsh, for bringing me to this beautiful country. Kathy Lette for opening up her platinum-plated address book and being a great mate, no matter how inter-continent we are.

Anthony Dennis, for having the excellent idea I might like to work at *The Sydney Morning Herald* (and being so great to work with). And John Alexander, another exceptional newspaper editor, for giving me the job, making me feel appreciated and for being so very good to me when my mother was ill.

Three more great editors: Jane Proctor and Dee Nolan for immense loyalty through illness and continental shifts. And my treasured friend Tyler Brûlé who came to see me in hospital when I had hardly any hair and still asked me to write for the grooviest magazine on the planet.

And some non-journos who deserve special mention:

Peter and Judy Howarth, for lending me their beautiful home, Wombramurra, complete with Zambia and Juica and Jake the kangaroo, where this book became one as opposed to several.

Darling Spikey Carr, for the gallery and all those years at Versailles. And Christian McCulloch, because I just love him.

At Penguin Books, Julie Gibbs, for believing in my squiggles as well as my doodads; Bob Sessions, for a wonderful tea at the Windsor Hotel; and Clare Forster, for being a New Romantic in Townsville, as well as for her dedicated professional attention.

And to my darling Popi for his neverfailing smile and support. Even when I was being a pizza.

All these pieces appeared first in *Good Weekend*, except 'Hats Off to Hats', 'Fat Chance', 'Shopping with Kate Moss', 'Oh Solo Me, Oh' and 'The Virus', which were published in *The Sydney Morning Herald* and are published with permission.